I0164770

Undoing the infallibility of "revealed knowledge" in Hinduism.

Selections from the translated "Introductory" notes of Hindu religious texts that were written in the 19th century by the Orientalists.

Open Windows: A Feminist Research Center.

This is a collaboration of Lies and Big Feet; an independent publishing house.

Copyright © 2016 Lies and Big Feet. Readers of these articles may copy them without the copyright owner's permission, if the author and publisher are acknowledged in the copy and copy is used for educational, not-for-profit purposes.

All rights reserved.

ISBN: 938428114X
ISBN-13: 978-9384281144

What we consider as infallible, sacred religious texts which comprise of "revealed knowledge" is actually a compilation of many texts and changes must have occurred in them through centuries, as they were handed down through generations.

CONTENTS

SECTION I: INTRODUCTION.

1   The Unstable Sacred Text.   1

2   Who gains with the advent of Print Culture?   7

SECTION II: EXTRACTS FROM THE "INTRODUCTIONS" OF THE TRANSLATED RELIGIOUS HINDU TEXTS.

1   VEDIC HYMNS.   45

2   HYMNS OF THE SAMAVEDA   68

3   THE SÁNKYA APHORISMS OF KAPILA   71

7   THE SACRED BOOKS OF THE EAST   79

INTRODUCTION

1 THE UNSTABLE SACRED TEXT.

Manuscripts of the Hindu religious texts were often transferred onto print in the early years of print culture in colonial Bengal, India, (i.e. during the last decades of the eighteenth century) under the aegis of the East India Company sponsored Orientalists, but what exactly were the processes involved? How did native-brahmins look upon it as they assisted the Britishers in making the shift take place from a manuscript culture to a realm of print technology?

In 1825, Graves Chamney Haughton, a professor of Hindu Literature in the East India College, published an out-of-print text, William Jones's translation of the Sanskrit *Manava Dharma Shastra* or the *Institutes of Manu*.[1] Sir William

---

[1] Throughout, I will be referring to *Manusmriti* and *Manavadharma*, synonymously. I will be using the following text: *Manavadharmasastra, or, The Institutes of Manu*, according to the Gloss of Kulluka, comprising the Indian system of Duties, Religious and Civil. Verbally translated from the original, with a Preface by Sir William Jones, and Collated with the Sanskrit Text, by Graves Chanmey Haughton, Esq., Professor of Hindu Literature in the East India College. THIRD EDITION, edited by The Revd. P. Percival, Professor of Vernacular Literature, Presidency College, Madras. (Madras,J.

Jones, an employee of the East India Company and referred to as the father of scientific linguistics and comparative philology, is a perfect example of a scholar who worked outside the Orientalist knowledge-making framework. He was also steeped in the culture of eighteenth century British print and had an immense trust in the veracity of printed texts. Haughton's prefatory note states that it was a new edition of Sir William Jones's translation; he writes that in his own text "the version of the learned translator has been carefully revised and compared" and that discrepancies would have been a result of the "variety of the manuscripts consulted by Sir William Jones." This observation provides us with historical documentation that there existed a "variety" of manuscripts that were consulted by these Orientalist scholars as they wrote their versions of the *Manusmriti*.

In 1794, the British government of India had Jones's *Manava Dharma* printed; Sir William Jones, writes in his preface about the processes involved in collaborating with the Brahmins in writing the text:

> ...[A]nd the brahman, who read it with me, requested most earnestly, that his name might be concealed; nor would he have read it for any consideration on a forbidden day of the moon,... so great, indeed, is the idea of sanctity annexed to this book, that, when the chief magistrate at Benaras endeavoured, at my request,

---

Higginbotham: 1863).

2

to procure a Persian translation of it, before I had a hope of being at any time able to understand the original, the Pandits of his court unanimously and positively refused to assist in the work; nor should I have procured it at all, if a wealthy Hindu at Gaya had not caused the version to be made by some of his dependants."

The question to ask is thus: did natives operate within a different parallel epistemic world where multiple manuscripts of the same text were seen as legitimate; moreover, why were the brahmins not necessarily keen to see their names on print, but neither were they hesitant to transfer a manuscript culture onto print? These early decades of colonial print can throw more light on the nature of religious-manuscripts that existed in India, before the advent of print in India. More importantly and is of relevance, is that: when we read a text like *Manusmriti*, why exactly should we assume that there exists an intact, untouched, version of the text?

Till as recently as two hundred years ago, India was a manuscript culture meaning that the printed text did not exist. When the transition took place from a manuscript culture to a print one, it seems to have taken place easelessly, implying that the shift was made without much murmurs and complaints from at least the native, elite sections of society. The Britishers, on the other hand, at seeing the beautiful manuscripts in Indian languages, must have been reminded of their pre-

print past and a lot of care was taken to ensure that these manuscripts were well kept. When Tipu Sultan lost the Mysore wars (1780-90s), his library was also taken and a concern was raised by the Company soldiers as to how the manuscripts were to be kept safe: "That part of the library of the late Tippoo Sultan, which was presented by the army to the Court of Directors, is lately arrived in Bengal; the Governor-General strongly recommends that the Oriental manuscripts composing this collection, should be deposited in the library of the College of Fort William, and it is his intention to retain the manuscripts accordingly, until he shall receive the orders of the Court upon the subject."[2] There was no rampant erasure of the Indian manuscript past, and in fact, the Company was keen to preserve this aspect of Indian culture.

---

[2] *The Annals of the College of Fort William, from the Period of its Foundation.*Arranged and Published by Thomas Roebuck, Calcutta, Printed by Philip Periera at the Hindoostanee Press, 1819. "Introduction" pp. xxv. The report mentions the importance of preserving old manuscripts: "The preservation and augmentation of the Collection of Eastern Manuscripts, afford the only means of arresting the progressive destruction of Oriental learning. Since the dismemberment of the Muslim, those works have been dispersed over India, and have been exposed to the injuries and hazards of time, accident and neglect. It is worthy of the ambition of this great Empire to employ every effort of its influence in preserving from destruction and decay, these valuable records of Oriental history, Science and Religion." p. 114.

The larger question, though, is: can we ever take it for a given that what we know, in a definitive manner, as being central to the Hindu *shastras* can be construed as being infallible? - for all we know – these texts might have been amended and changes made as they were handed down generations. In the preface to his version of *Manavadharma*, Sir William Jones wrote about the textual variations that existed and how he collated different versions that were available in manuscript form to arrive at his final text:[3]

> At length appeared KULLU'KA BHATTA; who, after a painful course of study and the collation of numerous manuscripts, produced a work, of which it may, perhaps, be said very truly, that it is the shortest, yet the most luminous, the least ostentatious, yet the most learned, the deepest, yet the most agreeable, commentary ever composed on any author [namely, Manu] ancient or modern, European or Asiatic. The Pandits care so little for genuine chronology, that none of them can tell me the age of KULLU'KA, whom they always name with applause; but he informs us himself, that he was a *Brahmin* of the *Varéndra* tribe, whose family had been long settled in *Gaur* or Bengal, but that he had chosen his residence among the learned on the banks of the holy river at Ka'si. His text and interpretation I have almost implicitly followed,

---

[3] *Manusmriti.*

> though I had myself collated many copies of
> MANU, and among them a manuscript of a very
> ancient date: …

We can arrive at the obvious conclusion that William Jones consulted many textual variations of the *Manusmriti*, and if so, the implication is that there was no single authoritative text. If these texts that constitute our Hindu *shastras* are unreliable with numerous variants existing simultaneously, then it stands to reason that there is no authentic version that we can refer to as being the original. Who is to tell as to which part comprised "revealed knowledge" and which sections were subsequent add-ons?

2 WHO GAINS WITH THE ADVENT OF PRINT?

A manuscript culture meant that religious texts were always spurious and quite unstable; what becomes evident is that different manuscripts had different versions of the same text. These religious texts also had commentaries which the scribe would have made. There is ample documentation on how these manuscripts were written; the East India Company scholars (in the 19th C.) and Western Orientalists who were involved in translating these religious texts have examined the variants that existed and how the manuscripts differed from each other. They keep on referring to how they had to "collate" different manuscripts and how these hand written texts had errors and side notes; the job of these Orientalist scholars was to come up with a perfect version of the text and have it printed - without errors. This, in turn, refers to the process of how manuscripts were written over the centuries in India; the implication is that the Brahmin pandits would have considered it a legitimate act to alter them and reinterpret these hand-written texts. Print technology was intrinsic to the processes of grammatical and textual standardization that took place in the 19th century due to the stringent measures taken by the British Orientalists, whereby the realm of a fluid manuscript culture was altered to allow for perfect texts to emerge; it also erased the editorial process where it was legitimate to constantly edit and amend religious manuscripts.

Metropole and center: the realm of print and empire making.

The specifics of the realm of print.

The realm of print was a complicit partner in the processes of empire making. When we consider how print was intrinsic to the formation of a colony by the East India Company, we are given a different perspective on the nature of how print entered India. In *Indian Ink, Script and Print in the Making of the English East India Company*,[4] Miles Ogborn looks at the importance of different modes of writing to the English East India Company in the seventeenth and eighteenth centuries, arguing that the company's world was "one made on paper as well as on land and sea."[5] Central to the book is the assumption that

---

[4] Miles Ogborn, *India Ink, Script and Print in the making of the English East India Company* (Chicago: University of Chicago Press, 1997).

[5] Ibid., p. xvii. What Ogborn wants to demonstrate is a way to look at the interconnections between imperial spaces, knowledge and power through "recent histories of reading, writing, and publishing." He goes on to argue that the operations and workings of power are found in the "concrete processes of the making, distribution, and use of texts as material objects. (pp. 5-6).

the "complexities of the exertion of power and the making of knowledge and profit in these mercantile and imperial worlds" are made evident in how different forms of writing were developed and deployed by the Company; thereby examining these texts can give us an insight in the connections between power and knowledge.[6] The correspondence of Robert Boyle,[7] the scientist who was also a member of the Court of Committees that managed the Company's operations, reveals that his world was also the "world of the English East India Company."[8] The leading scientific figures of England were involved in the processes of empire making (despite denying their monetary involvements), thus shifting the dynamics of how colonization took place – it was not a mere event of brutal force and gunpowder but the intellectual elite of England were involved and seemingly quite keen to disseminate knowledge.

The use of print in the colonies was not inevitable as manuscripts were used as well as handwritten notices and

---

[6] Ibid., p. xxi.

[7] Robert Boyle owned East India stock, and used his position in the Company to find jobs for those who used his patronage.

[8] Ibid., p. xvii. Boyle, though, was keen to emphasis that his involvement with the company was out of the desire for knowledge and not profit. Ogborn writes that historians of science consider Boyle's involvement in the seventeenth century scientific revolution and the foundation of the Royal Society to argue for a "conception of scientific knowledge that understands it as an engagement with political concerns that are inseparable from matters of practice." p.xxi.

circulars. Initially print was seen as a threat and many printers who attempted to print were deported to Europe. The works of Orientalist scholars are well known, but what need was there for grammar books and dictionaries to be printed and publicized and what part did the dissemination of printed material play in the debate of empire building in Bengal? Government patronage did determine the nature of print in the early years and for the publication of works on philology and grammar. [9] Patterns of dissemination and distribution were also determined by government finance.[10] Printed texts were circulated, enabling an imperial sphere of 'social communication' to be constructed that included readers and writers in India and in England, but this cannot necessarily be assumed to be a "consensual interpretative community"[11] for natives were not equal collaborators in this enterprise. These grammar books, legal texts and translations of religious texts were printed, placing them within an "imperial circuit" of production, dissemination and reception.[12] Moreover, the needs of empire building determined why grammar books were printed, and did not necessarily reflect the needs of the natives. Subsequently, these grammar books – meant to aid in standardizing Indian languages -- did become the definitive norm in India.

---

[9] Ibid., p. 220.

[10] Ibid., p. 221.

[11] Ibid., p. 223.

[12] Ibid., p. 225.

When examining the nature of how grammar books emerged in Calcutta, written on the same lines as grammar books in England, and the complicated logic behind them, it would be relevant to understand how grammar books evolved in England in a completely different context – or for that matter, how the emergence of the printing press helped in standardizing the English language. When William Caxton set up his printing press around 1476, it was about fifty years since the chancery English had been adopted as the standard, based on the London and the East Midland dialect. Caxton's press aided in making this dialect of English as the norm. Caxton set up his printing press in Westminister close to Parliament, and decided to print in the vernacular, realizing the economic prospects of the new venture. This was a smart move, as there had been other printers who had set up presses on Oxford and St. Albans, and had failed. These printers had published academic books in Latin, not realizing that such books could easily be available through trade with the Continent.[13]

It was largely for economic reasons that Caxton was searching for a "relatively stable language variety that could serve a superregional function to speakers of different dialects."[14] He used a dialect that was the most widely

---

[13] Norman Blake, *Caxton and his World* (London: Andre Deutsch,1969).

[14] Terttu Nevalainen and Ingrid Tieken-Boon van Ostade. "Standardisation," in *A History of the English Language*. eds. Richard Hogg and David Denison (Cambridge: Cambridge University Press, pp. 271-311; p. 278.

accepted written variety, and used by the literate segments of society, which constituted his own intended audience. By the end of the fifteenth century, "economic motivations contributed significantly to earlier linguistic and political ones in the standardization of the language."[15] Writing dictionaries and grammar books were some of the processes that were involved in standardizing a language. The first dictionaries were written in the early eighteenth century and were meant to include new, unfamiliar words that had entered the English language over the centuries; dictionaries were needed to explain these words to the common user or to the well educated[16] and did not include those words that were in everyday use. Nathan Bailey's *Dictionarium Britannicum*, that was written in 1730, was the first dictionary to include all words and was subsequently used as a source for Johnson's *Dictionary of the English Language* (1755).[17] Early grammarians resorted to Latin grammar to provide them with a model and English grammar was not considered as an object worthy of study for its own sake till 1653 with the publication of Wallis's *Grammatica Linguae Anglicanae*. English grammar was treated like Latin, and emphasis was given to its morphology. Grammarians of the eighteenth century wanted to fix the language, only to realize that a living language could not be fixed. Lindley Murray's grammar book (first published in

---

[15] Ibid., p. 278.

[16] Ibid., p. 283.

[17] Ibid., p. 284.

1795) came to be looked upon as a handbook of English grammar. English grammar books were taken as a model for grammar books on native languages and the need to write such books were driven by the needs of empire and the East India Company.

The nature of how these grammar books in the colonial context came to be written is symptomatic of Tony Ballantyne's argument that imperial knowledge was often disembodied from the socio-traditional context from within which they emerged. Ballantyne argues that colonial states gathered knowledge from a wide range of sources about the colonies and printing was crucial to the systematization and dissemination of colonial knowledge.[18] This form of codified knowledge was the basis of the day to day operation of colonial power, but "the processes by which they were created profoundly altered the knowledge they recorded, disembodying these traditions, wrenching them free of the traditional social contexts of knowledge transmissions to revalue them as an aid to the operation of imperial authority"[19] Recent histories of empire look at the connections between the role of colonial knowledge and the establishment of colonial authority.[20]

---

[18] Tony Ballantyne. "What Difference does Colonialism Make? Reassessing Print and Social Change in an age of global imperialism," in *Agent of Change: Print Culture Studies After Elizabeth L Eisenstein*, eds. Sabrina Baron, Eric Lindquist and Eleanor Shevlin (Amherst: University of Massachusets Press, 2007).

[19] Ibid., p. 345.

[20] As printing was "central" to the working of the modern colonial state, it has "become an important point of debate in the scholarship on modern empire

Even as colonial authorities used print to exercise power, what is not very clear is the nature of power? It is easy to write off colonial power as being absolute but power in this instance – as the preceding analysis has shown – was far from being totalitarian. Colonial authority did not operate in a binary of absolute coercion and pliant submission and the natives – for that matter, the intellectual elites in many instances – participated in the dissemination of colonial authority. Those who were being ruled allowed themselves to be a part of this process of technological exchange, even as it was used to make them subordinates.

East India Company Orientalism: the reasons behind the emergence of imperial print.

i. Economic imperatives and the East India Company

The realm of early print culture in Bengal was defined by the imperatives of empire and it would not have emerged the way it did if it had not been but for the economic support of the East India Company. We have to take into account the socio-historical and economic imperatives that determined the emergence of print culture in colonial Bengal. What are the socio-historical factors that determine how the "communications circuit" operated? In addition to

building"; print was an important tool for "colonial administrators, missionaries and social reformers" and was reconceptualized in the colonial situation. p. 343.

the "communications circuit" that involves the author, the publisher, the shipper, the bookseller and the reader, we have to consider their relation within the larger socio-historical and economic contexts. In this section, I examine the impetus behind the formation of imperial print and East India Company-sponsored scholarship, to argue that this body of work was created in order to sustain the empire.

The realm of early print before 1800, in Calcutta, still in its burgeoning stages and was meant primarily for the white settlers. 1800 marks a shift in the domain of print in Bengal as the year saw the establishment of two institutions, the Srirampur Missionary Press and the college of Fort William, where books, intended for the native population, were published under the auspices and patronage of the British government and Baptist missionaries. Disseminating books among the Indians would create an indigenous sphere of print culture, allowing the natives to engage with the materiality of the text, establish a reading public, and imbibe habits of reading, factors that would eventually enable the English to transmit European culture and ideas. Prior to the turn of the century, the realm of print culture was a closed circuit: all books, newspapers, gazettes, legal translations, in fact, all printed material had a very specific readership and catered to the practical, aesthetic and intellectual needs of the Europeans.

Tabulating the books that were printed before 1800, Graham Shaw categorizes the subjects that were dealt with:

translations from Persian and Sanskrit, literary and historical works, dictionaries, art works, travelogues, maps, Indian economics, works on religion, law, and military regulations. To a certain extent, this body of printed work written about India can be seen as contributing to a larger body of work that would become Orientalist scholarship, which according to Edward Said, was a "corporate institution dealing with the Orient."[21] For Said, the Orient came into being as a result of the printed narratives that were written about the East and filtered into the consciousness of Europe; these narratives were discursive constructs and distorted the material realities that they portrayed. A complete description of the "communications circuit" of printers, authors and booksellers remains incomplete if we fail to address the fact that it was partially driven by the needs of British empire. For example, a review of Nathaniel Halhed's *Grammar of the Bengal Language*[22] in the *English Review* in 1783 makes an easy equation between the study of Indian languages and its use in maintaining the British Empire in India.[23] The argument that is posited in the review is quite relevant in the present context: the aim of the British government was "to establish an empire over the minds as well as over the

---

[21] Edward Said, *Orientalism* (New York: Vintage, 1979).

[22] Nathaniel Halhed, *A Grammar of the Bengal Language*, 1778. Reprint, ed. R. C. Alston (England: The Scolar Press, 1969).

[23] "Review of Halhed's *Grammar of the Bengal Langauage*," *The English Review or An Abstract of Foreign and English Literature* 1(1783): 5-14.

country of the natives," and grammar books were needed to allow for an "easy" intercourse with the "native." The review states that the "languages of India" have been "totally disregarded by the Parliament and the Ministers of Britain; and they have been nearly as much neglected by the East India Direction"; it was because of the "literary zeal" of a "few private men" that progress was made in such studies and "Mr. Jones led the way" with his *Persian Grammar*, his *Poesis Asiatica Commentarii,* and other publications of erudition and elegance," followed by Mr. Richardson who also wrote "several works of ingenuity and research" particularly the *Dictionary of the Persian, Arabic, and English languages.*[24]

In fact, even the realm of print culture in Europe was partially determined by the institutions of empire and imperialism, as the public imagination of Georgian England was prolific with portrayals of imperial greatness and the colonies. Kathleen Wilson argues that images of empire permeated all aspects of domestic culture and politics.[25] Newspapers and periodical presses, even those that were the most apolitical, alongside with histories and topographies of the colonies "supported British superiority and power, fed the growing enthusiasm for the exotic and

---

[24] Ibid., pp. 5-6.

[25] Kathleen Wilson. "The Good, the Bad, and the Impotent: Imperialism and the Politics of Identity in Georgian England", in *The Consumption of Culture*, ed. Ann Bermingham and John Brewer (New York: Routledge, 1995), pp. 237-262.

the primitive, and legitimated British domination in terms comprehensible to the empire's domestic consumers [in England]."[26] The nature of the epistemological model that informed these portrayals of the empire is debatable; for Said, these representations of the Orient were fictive renditions of the Other and the writer-observers had little face-to-face interaction with the natives, while I would argue against such an assumption.

There was a sustained effort undertaken by the East India Company to ensure that there evolved a realm of print culture that contributed to imperial knowledge-making. The process of imperial knowledge-making did operate outside a dichotomous relationship of European active observer and native passive observed, and recent scholarship draws attention to such a model of analysis. Imperial knowledge-making, in fact, involved both natives and British scholars. Sir William Jones, referred to as the father of scientific linguistics and comparative philology, is a perfect example of a scholar who worked outside the Orientalist knowledge-making framework. He was also steeped in the culture of eighteenth century British print and had an immense trust in the veracity of printed texts. An employee of the East India Company, Jones examined Indian languages in order to make linguistic connections with European languages, drawing attention to the complexities of the local culture while also placing it on a

---

26 Ibid., p. 242.

"pattern of human history at a global level."[27] In his annual address to the Asiatic Society in Calcutta, which he founded, in February 1789, Jones described the Sanskrit language within a global context, stating; that "the Sanskrit language, whatever be its antiquity, is of a wonderful structure; [it is] more perfect than the Greek, more copious than the Latin, and more exquisitely refined than either, yet bearing to both of them a stronger affinity."[28] Jones had a very clear idea of how the Asiatic Society would operate, revealing an awareness that the process of Company-sponsored Orientalist knowledge construction would have to involve the natives. Jones makes it clear when he says:

> Much may … be expected from the communications of learned natives, whether lawyers, physicians, or private scholars, who should eagerly, on the first invitation, send us their … [works] on a variety of subjects…. . With a view to avail ourselves of this disposition, and to bring their latent science under our inspection, it might be advisable to print and circulate a short memorial, in Persian and Hindi … [advertising] the design of our institution. … To instruct others is the prescribed duty of learned

---

[27] Kapil Raj. "Refashioning Civilities, Engineering Trust: William Jones, Indian Intermediaries and the Production of Reliable Legal Knowledge in Late Eighteenth Century Bengal," *Studies in History* 17(2001): 23-47, 29.

[28] William Jones, *The Collected Works of Sir William Jones. 3 Vols.* (New York: New York University Press, 1993), *Vol. 3*, p. 34.

Brahmans, and, if they be men of substance, without reward; … and the Mahomedans have not only the permission, but the positive commands, of their law giver, to search for learning even in the remotest parts of the globe.[29]

In his address to the white diasporic community in Calcutta comprising scholar-administrators, Sir William Jones encourages them to be involved in the apparatuses of knowledge-gathering, laying out specific instructions as to how they were to work. They were to "contribute a succinct description of such manuscripts" as had been "perused or inspected, with their dates and the names of their owners, and to propose for solution such questions as had occurred to him concerning Asiatik Art, Science, and History, natural or civil"; subsequently, the Asiatic Society would "possess without labour, … a fuller catalogue of Oriental books."[30] It was through a collaborative process, dependant on a relationship between the scholar and natives, that a catalogue of Oriental books could be established. Jones was implementing the strictures of British eighteenth century print culture, evident in his valorization of print technology as against manuscript culture.

---

[29] Jones, *Collected Works, Vol. 3*, pp. 21-22.

[30] Ibid., pp. 21-22.

In order to contribute to this realm of print culture, there were specific methods and methodologies that informed how the books were to be printed and written. A zone of contact was to be created so that the natives would trust the East India Company scholars and impart their knowledge; this process of imperial knowledge making was an act of intellectual engagement. In many ways, William Jones displays an attitude in keeping with the notion of gentlemanly etiquette that marked the European seventeenth century scientific community on how experiments were to be conducted. Drawing upon the arguments of Steven Shapin that notions of "trust" and civility" were dominant attitudes that defined the nature of scientific experiments in seventeenth century England, Kapil Raj arrives at a similar conclusion in his examination of the works of William Jones, stating that it was a "new, hybrid regime of knowledge, organizing and disciplining both Indian and British functionaries" and introduced a sense of "security, loyalty, and hierarchy."[31] I would shy away from describing this new colonial "hybrid" system of imperial knowledge-making as operating within benevolent spaces of intellectual engagement. Even when face-to-face contact took place between the white rulers and the natives, there was an uneven structure of power that marked these encounters despite the element of civility. In most instances, with changes in the local, native patronages, where local rulers suffered under the political interventions

---

[31] Raj, "Refashioning Civilities," p. 20.

of the East India Company-state, disrupting indigenous institutions of learning, the educated natives were compelled to impart knowledge to the white scholar-administrators of the East India Company in order to survive. There was a fracture between William Jones' private affinity, admiration and loyalty to Asiatic culture and his inevitable public role as intelligencer, surveyor and enumerator of the Raj.

The scholarship of Sir William Jones can be considered Company Orientalism and emerged only after 1780. Sanskrit, as a language, was till then, an enigma and remained elusive to Europeans. Sanskrit was seen as having the keys to a vast store of Indian knowledge, but there were very few who would help the Britishers learn the language. Most educated Hindus were hesitant to engage with Europeans and communicate to them any aspects of their own religion. But towards the end of the eighteenth century, with the rise of the East India Company as rulers, Orientalist scholarship as a disciplinary institution came into being under the patronage of the scholar-administrators of the Company. The East India Company substituted for native patronages of learning, and with the decline of the native aristocracies, many Brahmin scholars became destitute and gradually had to accept positions imparting knowledge to the new rulers.[32] For Sir William Jones, native scholars were to be used, but were never to be

[32] Tony Ballantyne, *Orientalism and Race: Aryanism in the British Empire* (New York: Palgrave, 2002), pp. 1-55.

considered as intrinsic to the mission. For example, Jones wanted to admit natives into the Asiatic society but was unsure as to how his proposal would be received by the other Britishers. He compiled translations of Hindu and Muslim Laws in order to aid the "benevolent intentions of the legislature of Great Britain,"[33] using the knowledge of the "most learned Hindus and Mohammedans."[34] There was little "amusement" in working on these translations, except the belief and desire of "rendering his knowledge useful to his nation, and beneficial to the inhabitants of these provinces."[35] Company Orientalism, unlike Said's Foucault-inspired version of Orientalism, emerged as a result of the close interaction between the natives and the Europeans and can be described as a detailed and organized body of knowledge fashioned by the East India Company in the late eighteenth century.[36]

---

[33] Jones, *Complete Works, Vol. 3*, p. vi.

[34] Ibid., p. vii.

[35] Ibid., p. vii.

[36] Central to Company Orientalism was a Sanskrito-centric vision of India that celebrated Sanskrit and the ancient past, but decried contemporary culture as debased. This attitude was in keeping with the eighteenth century fascination with the classical languages and literatures making the British believe that the ancient Hindus, like the Greeks and the Romans, had created a culture that was lost as a result of the medieval dark ages. Jones was much aware of the dichotomy within which he was operating, as he wrote, "Whoever travels in Asia, especially if he conversant with the literature of the countries through which he passes, must naturally remark on the superiority of European talents" (Jones, *Complete Works, Vol. 3*, p.

The power of this realm of print culture is evident in the fact that it enabled to maintain control over the colonial territories. As early as 1783, a review appeared in an English journal, which when describing the need for grammar books and language books on the natives said that "without an easy and general intercourse with the natives, through the medium of language, no system of regulation … can promote any solid, rational or permanent establishment of authority and power" as no people could "cheerfully submit to rulers" they did not understand."[37] More importantly, the cultivation of this kind of imperial print was a sustained effort and in keeping with the East India Company policies; the Company's trading success was a result of the scientific revolution of the seventeenth century and the institution had eminent scientists of the Royal Society, like Robert Boyle, Isaac Newton, Joseph Banks as its directors or major shareholders. Not surprisingly, Company Orientalism had a small but influential readership, a sphere of print communication that informed the practices of empire formation. The body of Orientalist work that emerged from India in the late eighteenth century and influenced European notions of the colonies was a result of print capital. The works of the

12). As "minute geographical knowledge "was needed" so was the knowledge of the "natural productions of these territories, especially in the vegetable and mineral systems" as these were "momentous objects of research to an imperial" and "commercial people" (Ibid., pp. 13-14).

[37] "Review of Halhed's Grammar Book," *The English Review, or, An Abstract of English and Foreign Literature* 1(1783): 5-14, 5.

Calcutta based Orientalists were widely disseminated in Europe as a result of Jones' letter writing and print culture.[38] The "communications circuit" was immense, spreading across continents. A single author, located in India, had books printed in India and England and these were translated and read by a European audience.

ii. The characteristics of Western print

Empire making was made possible through the realm of print culture. Not only was the technology transferred, but so were the socially ascribed characteristics of print. Sir William Jones, operating within the ideology of eighteenth century print culture that associated print with truth, assumed that the technology of print had the power to transform a pre-modern, Indian scribal culture into western modernity. But this equation between print and truth was not intrinsic to letterpress technology as till the early decades of the eighteenth century there was a suspicion of the printed word. In *The Nature of the Book: Print and Knowledge in the Making*, Adrian Johns draws attention to assumptions about print culture, stating that what we "often regard as essential elements and necessary concomitants of print are in fact rather more contingent than generally acknowledged. Veracity in particular is … extrinsic to the press itself, and has had to be grafted onto

---

[38] Ballantyne, *Orientalism and Race*, pp. 1-55.

it."[39] A printed book could never be trusted to be what it claimed. Johns claims that in the seventeenth century, piracy and plagiarism were dominant fears. It was a matter of routine that books could be considered dubious; therefore, it was impossible to trust any printed report. Pirate editions of Shakespeare, Donne and Sir Thomas Browne were liable to egregious errors, and so was Sir Isaac Newton's unauthorized publication of *Principia* and the first scientific journal, the *Philosophical Transactions*. It was only in 1760 that the first book was printed without any errors.

Not surprisingly, till early in the eighteenth century, print was seen as suspect, without any intrinsic characteristic of truth. Printers, booksellers and authors, who gained the most commercially, put forward the notion of the truth and superiority of print in contrast to manuscripts. If print culture was to be a viable economical institution, a "communications circuit" involving the author, publisher, the printer, the shipper, the book-seller, and the reader had to be in harmonious coexistence, with the reader believing in the veracity of print. Writers were often propagandists of print, as much as theorists, and this is how Paula McDowell describes Daniel Defoe, the eighteenth century's "most prolific printed author," who wrote in his *Essay upon Literature* (1726), "The Printing Art has out-run the Pen, and may pass for the greatest improvement of its Kind in

---

[39] Adrian Johns, *The Nature of the Book: Print and Knowledge in the Making* (Chicago: University of Chicago Press, 2000), p. 2.

the World."[40] All of Defoe's writings imply that the oral past should be, but is not, cut off from the print-oriented present and future. Regarding Defoe's historical fiction, *A Journal of the Plague Year* (1772), McDowell points out that the text moves diachronically in time as the present modern age of print was a move away from the backward past associated with oral culture. Defoe also moves "synchronically across different communicative modes that in reality are coexisting and interdependent" but are represented as parts of a "linear, progressive development."[41] Defoe's printed books contribute to an "emergent model of a hierarchy of forms of communication with print at its apex"[42] as the writer attempts to draw an equation, not existing before, between print and "enhanced fidelity, reliability, and truth."[43] In this process, orality is relegated to the realm of old wives tales.

By the time of Sir William Jones, England had become an increasingly print-oriented society, shifting away from its oral past. This explains Jones' feverish desire to transcribe every manuscript into print, as the process would lend an element of fixity to unstable scribal texts. In an

---

[40] Paula McDowell, "Defoe and the Contagion of the Oral: Modeling Media Shift in A Journal of the Plague Year," *PMLA* 121(1): 87-106.

[41] Ibid., p. 88.

[42] Ibid., p. 89.

[43] Johns, *The Nature of the Book*, p. 5.

advertisement in *The Calcutta Gazette*, in 1789, Sir William Jones wrote:

> The correctness of modern Arabian and
> Persian Books is truly deplorable, nothing can
> preserve them in any degree of accuracy but
> the art of printing; and if Asiatic literature
> should ever be general, it must diffuse itself,
> as Greek learning was diffused in Italy after
> the taking of Constantinople, by mere
> impressions of the best manuscripts without
> versions or comments, which future scholars
> would add at their leisure to future editions:
> but no printer should engage in so expensive a
> business without the patronage and the purse
> of monarchs of states, or society of wealthy
> individuals or at least without a large public
> subscription.[44]

Jones was extremely conscious of entering a realm of scribal culture in Bengal, and this is reflected in his desire to constantly transfer manuscripts into printed texts. In a way, by transferring written texts into print, his central aim was to codify knowledge, and in the process allow for control of what was disseminated about India. In 1768, before Jones sailed for India, he wrote to Count Revicski, the

---

[44] William Jones, *The Calcutta Gazette*, October 29, 1789.

Imperial Minister of Warsaw, describing the difficulties that were present when trying to locate a single meaning in manuscripts; it was "impossible to find two manuscripts [of Oriental literature] without error," he wrote, and "it was "absolutely necessary … to possess two copies of every one" which he would read so that "faults of the one" would be "corrected by the other."[45] In many of his letters, Jones voices a similar concern, where he reveals an intense desire to transcribe everything that he reads into print. Writing to one Dr. Patrick Russel in 1786, he said, "I congratulate you on the completion of your two works, but exhort you to publish them."[46] Jones goes on to say, "think how much fame Koenig lost by delaying his publications" and even if printing is "dear at Calcutta," if "government" printed Russel's works, he would "cheerfully superintend commas and colons."[47] A year later, Jones voices a similar concern in another letter,

> I have just read a very old book on that art [of music] in Sanskrit. I hope to present the world with the substance of it, as soon as the transactions of our society [The Asiatic Society] can be printed; but we go slowly, since the press is often engaged by government; … The *Asiatik Miscellany*, to which you

---

[45] Jones, *Complete Works, Vol. 1*, p. 101.

[46] Jones, *Complete Works, Vol. 2*, p. 99.

[47] Ibid., pp. 100-101.

allude, is not the publication of our society, who mean to print no scraps, nor any *mere* translations. It was the undertaking of a private gentleman, and will certainly be of use in diffusing Oriental literature, though it has [not?] been so correctly printed as I could wish.[48]

Manuscripts are seen as being less than perfect while printed texts allow for true, correct knowledge to emerge. Print technology is invested with a kind of truth power that is denied to manuscripts. Power resides in the capacity to be able to use print, and in the process, to make it accessible to larger groups of people. Mechanical reproducibility, made possible as a result of letterpress technology, would make knowledge more reproducible but also more authentic. The realm of print spread across continents, and made it possible to control the colonial territories.

The East India Company was interested in documenting all forms of knowledge that it could lay its hands on and supported many such works; all grammar books and translations were justified as they could help in empire building. Translations of historical and administrative works were seen as essential in carrying out the operations of the Company, and often, these works were partially

---

[48] Ibid., pp. 123-124.

subscribed and recommended by the East India Company. For example, Francis Gladwin's translation of Abu al-Fazl Ibn Mubarak's *Ayeen Akbery* was published in 1783, and seen as an endeavor that would serve the company as the "work comprehends the original constitution of the Mogul Empire, described under the immediate inspection of its founder; and will serve to assist the judgment of the Court of Directors."[49] In the introduction to the translation, there is a lengthy explanation of how the text would be beneficial to the company: "It will show where the measures of their administration approach to the first principles, which perhaps will be found superior to any that have been built on their ruins, and certainly most easy, as the most familiar to the minds of the people, and when any deviation from them may be likely to counteract, or to assimilate with them."[50] The third volume contained a "full account of the religion of the Hindoos; their books and the subjects of them: their several sects and the points in which they differ."[51] There were astronomical notes which were provided by Reuben Burrow, who applied with "great diligence to the study of the Sanskrit language" and also made a "perfect knowledge of Hindoo astronomy."[52] The

---

[49] *Ayeen Akbery: or The Institutes of the Emperor Akber, Vol. I.* trans. by Francis Gladwin, pp. xi-xii. 1783.

[50] Ibid., p. xi-xii.

[51] The "Preface" to *Ayeen Akbery, Vol. III.* trans. by Francis Gladwin. Printed by William Mackay, Calcutta Gazette Press, 1786.

[52] Ibid.

Governor General and Council recommended to the Court of Director the purchase of one hundred and fifty copies of the first edition of the *Ayeen Akbery*; this was, after all, a "work which may prove of the utmost utility to the Company, as it contains the original Institutes of the Sultan Akber, the founder of the empire."[53] Company patronage did provide a much needed monetary impetus for native types to be developed and these were subsequently used by the natives.

Grammar Books and print culture

Grammar books on Indian languages were meant to aid the East India Company. In order to maintain order in the colonies, it was essential to learn the languages of the Indians; this territorial domain of the colonies could be controlled by mastering the realm of native languages and codifying them in grammar books. Grammar books like Francis Gladwin's *The Persian Moonshe* (1795), *A Vocabulary, Persian, Arabic, and English* (1797), which aided the British to learn Persian and Bengali, were printed by English printing presses to cater to the needs of the administrators of the Company. This realm of texts was specific to the English community in Calcutta, and was meant to aid in trade and rule. Such texts play a similar role as that of colonial

---

[53] *Fort William-India House Correspondence, vol. IX, 1782-85*, edited by B.A. Saletore, Delhi, 1959. Also Gladwin's "Preface" to *Ayeen Akbery, Vol. II*, p. iii.

cartography in the processes of British empire building. As Ian Barrow argues, the mapping of India and the creation of colonial territory helped to build British national identity.[54] Colonial cartography depicted histories of British territorial possession and these histories helped the British to remake themselves as legitimate rulers while also reinforcing the notion of a British national identity. Grammar books, for the most, made colonial possession more legitimate. One of the first books to be written was Nathaniel Halhed's *A Grammar of the Bengal Language*, in 1778. In 1783, a reviewer in *The English Review* wrote that the "settlements in the East" deserve the "chief attention" of Britain. A printed grammar book would draw public attention to the language spoken by "millions of industrious British subjects" and would also aid in the "proper management of the commercial, military and revenue departments in Bengal."[55]

Printing a grammar book would allow for better communication between the government and the natives, enabling benevolent rule. Print was an extension of the state and the state defined itself through print. For Halhed:

---

[54] Ian Barrow, *Making History, Drawing Territory. British Mapping in India, c. 1756-1905* (New Delhi: Oxford University Press, 2003).

[55] "Review of Halhed's *A Grammar of the Bengal Language*", *The English Review*, p. 5-14.

The wisdom of the British Parliament has within these few years taken a decisive part in the internal policy and civil administration of its Asiatic territories…. Much however still remains for the completion of this grand work; and we may reasonably presume, that one of its most important desiderata is the cultivation of a right understanding and of a general medium of intercourse between Government, and its subjects; between the natives of Europe who are to rule, and the Inhabitants of India who are to obey.[56]

If the British were to rule, then print would play an important function in making that rule possible. Halhed draws a comparison between the present British conquest of Bengal and the colonial desire to learn the language of the natives with a historical antecedent, when the Romans, " a people of little learning and less taste, [who] had no sooner conquered Greece than they applied themselves to the study of Greek."[57] Learning the language of Bengal would allow the rulers to explain the benevolent principles of that Legislation whose decrees they enforce[d]"; the desire was to "convince" and persuade the natives" while

[56] Halhed, *A Grammar*, pp. i-ii

[57] Ibid., p. 1.

they commanded.[58] The economic imperatives were enormous and would be no less beneficial to the Revenue Department.[59] In all respects, the printed grammar book was a means of inevitable social progress.

Territorial control was possible because of the scientific and technological advancement of England. A similar argument is made in *Mapping an Empire: The Geographical Construction of British India, 1765-1843*, where Matthew Edney argues that that the extensive trigonometrical surveys conducted in southern and central India in the nineteenth century encouraged many Britishers to believe that they knew the real India.[60] Trigonometrical surveys had the power to depict land in a precise manner and the ideal of scientific, rational depiction was a contrast to the ineffectual and non-rational Indians and the non-elite sections of British society who were caricatured as ineffectual and not capable of sustained rational thought. The power of trigonometrical mapping, with its seemingly objective and scientific nature, permitted the British administrators to believe that these cartographic portrayals could capture the real India, and demonstrate the superiority of the British. The maps portrayed more than land; they depicted totalizing power and knowledge. The

---

[58] Ibid., pp. i-ii.

[59] Ibid., p. xv.

[60] Matthew Edney, *Mapping an Empire. The Geographical Construction of British India, 1765-1843* (Chicago: University of Chicago Press, 1999).

belief behind print technology was that the Western disciplinary institutions could control the colonies.

By the latter part of the eighteenth century, print culture was seen as being superior to other forms of communication. The move was towards codifying into print all the existing knowledge systems documented in a scribal-manuscript culture and this was construed as a shift into inevitable progress. Halhed draws attention to the mechanical aspects of print technology. The book, he writes, was to be seen as "extraordinary" and an "instance of mechanic abilities" and meant for the British public whose "curiosity" would be "strongly excited by the beautiful characters" that were displayed in the text.[61] Making Bengali fonts was not easy as the Bengali letters were "very difficult to be imitated in steel." Halhed erroneously credits Mr. Wilkins, an employee of the East India Company as being successful by undertaking the various occupations of "Metallurgist, the Engraver, the Founder and the Printer,"[62] and completely misrepresents the fact that natives were also involved; in fact, Panchanan Karmakar played an important role along with Wilkins. The process that was involved, of creating types in steel, of transferring and establishing clarity to the illegible, handwritten manuscripts—where the "inaccuracy of their writings" frequently deviated from their original forms— imparted a sense of authenticity and fixity to the act of

---

[61] Halhed, *A Grammar*, p. xxiii.

[62] Ibid., p. xxiv.

writing.[63] Technology is celebrated as it has the capacity to represent even the most difficult of languages. Print technology made pure the existing state of social affairs; the various "impositions and forgeries with which Bengal at present abounds," Halhed wrote, would be done away with.[64]

Halhed has to be seen as working within the existing ideological notions of empire-making. Britain defined itself as civilized and modern by characterizing India and its languages as primitive. British rule was conceived as benevolent, a system of government, made possible and facilitated through print unlike scribal culture. The British nation was interested in "marking the progress of her conquests by a liberal communication of Arts and Sciences, rather than by the effusion of blood."[65] The "poorer classes of people" were oppressed in a "country still fluctuating between the relics of former despotic dominion, and the liberal spirit of its present legislature."[66] To "enforce stability" in the British empire and in order for the administration to gain in "popularity," the "discouraged husbandman, the neglected artist, and oppressed laborer" would seek "asylum" in British "territories."[67] Print

---

[63] Ibid., p .3.

[64] Ibid., p. xxiv.

[65] Ibid., p. xxv.

[66] Ibid., p. xvi.

[67] Ibid., p. xvi.

technology possessed all the rational and benevolent characteristics of the English government; the "vigour" and "impartiality" that marked the operations of the government were seen in the printed grammar book. Moreover, Halhed defines how the Bengali language was to be, and attempts to cleanse it, by doing away with "foreign" influences[68] and by presenting the Bengali language as "derived from its parent the Sanskrit";[69] words that were not "natives of the country are not a part of his text and he has only selected the "most authentic and ancient compositions."[70] The study of the language, Halhed argued, was made difficult due to the "carelessness and ignorance of the people"; it had many "anomalous characters" and deviations from the "original forms" giving rise to spurious characters.[71] The existing state of Bengali, as a language, was representative of the natives: lacking a sense of coherence and uniformity. Language and culture are imbued with characteristics of a nation; the natives are emasculated and deviant, awaiting British colonization, akin to the fact that this scribal culture awaited print culture for progress. The spatial realm of the communications circuit mimics and replicates the ideologies of the political.[72]

---

[68] Ibid., p. xx.

[69] Ibid., p. xxi.

[70] Ibid., p. xxii.

[71] Ibid., p. 3.

[72] Vidyasagar was to echo this criticism fifty years later.

Halhed was operating within existing Western ideologies where the British nation was construed as masculine in contrast to the effeminate colonies. Mrinalini Sinha makes a similar argument in *Colonial Masculinity: The "Manly Englishman" and the "Effeminate Bengali" in the Late Nineteenth Century*, when she states that the social constructs of the manly Englishman and the effeminate Bengali in nineteenth-century India were a result of the emerging dynamics between colonial and nationalist politics and "is best captured in the logic of colonial masculinity."[73] The contours of colonial masculinity were shaped in the context of an "imperial social formation that included both Britain and India."[74] The figures of the "manly Englishman" and the "effeminate Bengali *babu*," according to Sinha, "were produced by, and helped to shape, the shifts in the political economy of colonialism in the late nineteenth century."[75] Though Sinha analyses nineteenth century colonial Bengal, the ideological contrasts of British masculinity and colonial effeminacy can be traced back to a hundred years ago, as Halhed makes clear.

There is nothing intrinsic to print for the technology to be considered as masculine and rational in comparison to manuscript texts. The characteristics of masculinity were

---

[73] Mrinalini Sinha, *Colonial Masculinity: The 'Manly Englishman' and the 'Effeminate Bengali' in the Late Nineteenth Century* (New York: St. Martin's Press, 1995), p. 1.

[74] Ibid., p. 2.

[75] Ibid., p. 3.

socially ascribed to printed texts. In the early modern period in England, for example, writers were hesitant to see their works being printed, or to be seen ideologically and physically as involved in the marketplace of printers and publication. For the female writer, Jody Greene argues, publication was akin to prostitution, while the male writers shared this anxiety more acutely.[76] The act of publication, that is, submitting one's works to the press, made the writer vulnerable to charges of sexual deviance and indecent exposure. "The male writer," according to Wendy Wall, "always trades on his vulnerability when he agrees to play the female role and be 'pressed' for the public."[77] By the seventeenth century, in England, increased literacy, the growth of cities and the flow of international capital improved print technology, and authors were more willing to make public works that would have a century ago been limited to private consumption. This caused an explosion in the number of printed books, doing away with how print was conceived. In eighteenth century England, print was seen at the apex of the communication system. For Halhed, writing in 1783, print was imbued with all the characteristics of the British nation and construed as vigorous, rational and truthful.

---

[76] Jody Greene, "Francis Kirkman's Counterfeit Authority: Autobiography, Subjectivity, Print," *PMLA* 121(1): 17-32.

[77] Wendy Wall, *The Imprint of Gender: Authority and Publication in the English Renaissance* (Ithaca, Cornell UP, 1993), p. 182.

Scribal-manuscript culture, on the other hand, was defined as archaic and not very reliable. Halhed represents these elements of inauthenticity as inherent in the behavioural habits of the natives, stating that it was with "obstinate and inviolable obscurity the Jentoos conceal … the Mysteries of their faith."[78] This particular grammar text, like other books printed by the scholar-administrators of the East India Company, would undo by making public the concealment, "obscurity" and archaic-ness of scribal knowledge. Halhed was engaged in revealing the knowledge systems that were "shut up in the libraries of Brahmins,"[79] and in undoing the "impenetrable reserve" of the Hindus.[80] While describing the efforts that were taken to write the grammar book, he says that he followed a very clear "set of rules" and in as "comprehensive" a manner as he could "devise" but the "task was rendered very laborious by the great multiplicity of observations" that he had collected.[81] For Halhed, modern print capitalism would give "a new fixity to language" allowing for a sense of "antiquity" of language" central to the formation of a modern consciousness.[82] Therefore, the realm of print culture

---

[78] Halhed, *A Grammar*, p. x.

[79] Ibid., p. iii.

[80] Ibid., p. xi.

[81] Ibid., pp. xviii-xix.

[82] Benedict Anderson. *Imagined Communities. Imagined Communities: Reflections on the Origin and Spread of Nationalism* (New York: Verso, 1991), p. 44.

mimics the ideological realm of the political, making colonial rule possible.

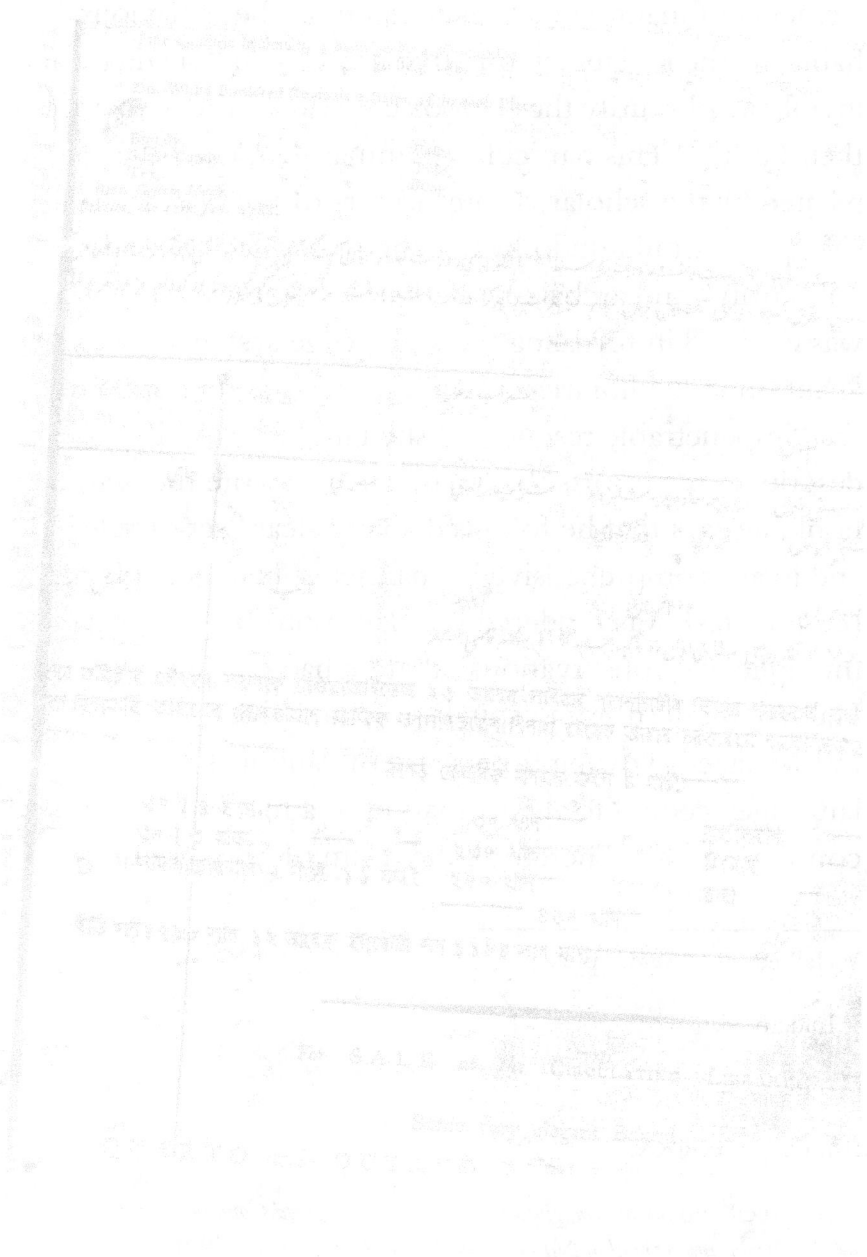

PART II:
EXTRACTS FROM THE "INTRODUCTIONS" OF THE TRANSLATED RELIGIOUS HINDU TEXTS.

I

VEDIC HYMNS

PART I

HYMNS TO THE MARUTS, RUDRA, VÂYU, AND VÂTA

Translated by

F. MAX MÜLLER

Clarendon: Oxford University Press

[1891]

Introduction.

...

And there is this additional difficulty that when we deal with inscriptions, we have at all events the text as it was engraved from the first, and we are safe against later modifications and interpolations, while in the case of the Veda, even though the text as presupposed by the Prâtisâkhyas may be considered as authoritative for the fifth century B.C., how do we know what changes it may have undergone before that time? Nor can I help giving expression once more to misgivings I have so often expressed, whether the date of the Prâtisâkhyas is really beyond the reach of doubt, and whether, if it is, there is no other way of escaping from the conclusion that the whole collection of the hymns of the Rig-veda, including even the Vâlakhilya hymns, existed at that early time. The more I study the hymns, the more I feel staggered at the conclusion at which all Sanskrit scholars seem to have arrived, touching their age. That many of them are old, older than anything else in Sanskrit, their grammar, if nothing else, proclaims in the clearest way. But that some of them are modern imitations is a conviction that forces itself even on the least sceptical minds. Here too we must guard against positivism, and suspend our judgment, and accept correction with a teachable spirit. No one would be more grateful for a way out of the maze of Vedic chronology than I should be, if a more modern date could be assigned to some of the Vedic hymns than the period of the rise of Buddhism. But how can we account for Buddhism without Vedic hymns? In the oldest Buddhist Suttas the hymns of three Vedas are constantly referred to, and warnings are uttered even against the fourth Veda, the Âthabbana. The Upanishads also, the latest productions of the Brâhmana period, must have been known to the founders of Buddhism. From all this there seems to be no escape, and yet I must confess that my conscience quivers in assigning such compositions as the Vâlakhilya hymns to a period preceding the rise of Buddhism in India.

PREFACE

TO THE FIRST EDITION.

WHEN some twenty years ago I decided on undertaking
the first edition of the two texts and the commentary of
the Rig-veda, I little expected that it would fall to my
lot to publish also what may, without presumption, be
called the first translation of the ancient sacred hymns
of the Brahmans. Such is the charm of deciphering
step by step the dark and helpless utterances of the
early poets of India, and discovering from time to time
behind words that for years seemed unintelligible, the
simple though strange expressions of primitive
thought and primitive faith, that it required no small
amount of self-denial to decide in favour of devoting a
life to the publishing of the materials rather than to
the drawing of the results which those materials
supply to the student of ancient language and ancient
religion. Even five and twenty years ago, and without
waiting for the publication of Sâyana's commentary,
much might have been achieved in the interpretation
of the hymns of the Rig-veda. With the MSS. then
accessible in the principal libraries of Europe, a
tolerably correct text of the Samhitâ might have been
published, and these ancient relics of a primitive
religion might have been at least partially deciphered
and translated in the same way in which ancient
inscriptions are deciphered and translated, viz. by a
careful collection of all grammatical forms, and by a

complete intercomparison of all passages in which the same words and the same phrases occur. When I resolved to devote my leisure to a critical edition of the text and commentary of the Rig-veda rather than to an independent study of that text, it was chiefly from a conviction that the traditional interpretation of the Rig-veda, as embodied in the commentary of Sâya*n*a and other works of a similar character, could not be neglected with impunity, and that sooner or later a complete edition of these works would be recognised as a necessity. It was better therefore to begin with the beginning, though it seemed hard sometimes to spend forty years in the wilderness instead of rushing straight into the promised land.

It is well known to those who have followed my literary publications that I never entertained any exaggerated opinion as to the value of the traditional interpretation of the Veda, handed down in the theological schools of India, and preserved to us in the great commentary of Sâya*n*a. More than twenty years ago, when it required more courage to speak out than now, I expressed my opinion on that subject in no ambiguous language, and was blamed for it by some of those who now speak of Sâya*n*a as a mere drag in the progress of Vedic scholarship. Even a drag, however, is sometimes more conducive to the safe advancement of learning than a whip; and those who recollect the history of Vedic scholarship during the last five and twenty years, know best that, with all its faults and weaknesses, Sâya*n*a's commentary was a sine quâ non for a scholarlike study of the Rig-veda. I do not wonder that others who have more recently entered on that study are inclined to speak disparagingly of the scholastic interpretations of Sâya*n*a. They hardly know how much we all owe to his guidance in effecting our first entrance into this fortress of Vedic language and Vedic religion, and how much even they, without being aware of it, are indebted to that Indian Eustathius. I do not withdraw an opinion which I expressed many years ago, and for which I was much blamed at the time, that Sâya*n*a in many cases teaches us how the Veda ought not to be, rather than how it ought to be understood. But for all that, who does not know how much assistance may be derived from a first translation, even though it is imperfect, nay, how often the very mistakes of our predecessors help us in finding the right track? If now we can walk without Sâya*n*a, we ought to bear in mind that five and twenty years ago we could not have made even our first steps, we could never, at least, have gained a firm footing without his leading strings. If therefore we can now see further than he could, let us not forget that we are standing on his shoulders.

I do not regret in the least the time which I have devoted to the somewhat tedious work of editing the commentary of Sâya*n*a, and editing it according to the strictest rules of critical scholarship. The Veda, I feel convinced, will occupy scholars for centuries to come, and will take and maintain for ever its position as the most ancient of books in the library of mankind. Such a book, and the commentary of such a book, should be edited once for all; and unless some unexpected discovery is made of more ancient MSS., I do not anticipate that any future Bekker or Dindorf will find much to glean for a new edition of Sâya*n*a, or that the text, as restored by me from a collation of the best MSS. accessible in Europe, will ever be materially shaken. It has taken a long time, I know; but those who find fault with me for the delay, should remember that few scholars, if any, have worked for others more than I have done in copying and editing Sanskrit texts, and that after all one cannot give up the whole of one's life to the collation of Oriental MSS. and the correction of proof-sheets. The two concluding volumes have long been ready for Press, and as soon as I can find leisure, they too shall be printed and published.

...

After these preliminary remarks I have to say a few words on the general plan of my translation.

I do not attempt as yet a translation of the whole of the Rig-veda, and I therefore considered myself at liberty to group the hymns according to the deities to which they are addressed. By this process, I believe, a great advantage is gained. We see at one glance all that has been said of a certain god, and we gain a more complete insight into his nature and character. Something of the same kind had been attempted by the original collectors of the ten books, for it can hardly be by accident that each of them begins with hymns addressed to Agni, and that these are followed by hymns addressed to Indra. The only exception to this rule is the eighth Ma*nd*ala, for the ninth being devoted to one deity, to Soma, can hardly be accounted an exception. But if we take the Rig-veda as a whole, we find hymns, addressed to the same deities, not only scattered about in different books, but not even grouped together when they occur in one and the same book. Here, as we lose nothing by giving up the old arrangement, we are surely at liberty, for our own purposes, to put together such hymns as have a common object, and to place before the reader as much material as possible for an exhaustive study of each individual deity.

I give for each hymn the Sanskrit original in what is known as the Pada text, i. e. the text in which all words (pada) stand by themselves, as they do in Greek or Latin, without being joined together according to the rules of Sandhi. The text in which the words are thus joined, as they are in all other Sanskrit texts, is called the Saṃhitâ text. Whether the Pada or the Saṃhitâ text be the more ancient, may seem difficult to settle. As far as I can judge, they seem to me, in their present form, the product of the same period of Vedic scholarship. The Prâtisâkhyas, it is true, start from the Pada text, take it, as it were, for granted, and devote their rules to the explanation of those changes which that text undergoes in being changed into the Saṃhitâ text. But, on the other hand, the Pada text in some cases clearly presupposes the Saṃhitâ text. It leaves out passages which are repeated more than once, while the Saṃhitâ text always repeats these passages; it abstains from dividing the termination of the locative plural su, whenever in the Saṃhitâ text, i. e. according to the rules of Sandhi, it becomes shu; hence nadîshu, agishu, but ap-su; and it gives short vowels instead of the long ones of the Saṃhitâ, even in cases where the long vowels are justified by the rules of the Vedic language. It is certain, in fact, that neither the Pada nor the Samhitâ text, as we now possess them, represents the original text of the Veda. Both show clear traces of scholastic influences. But if we try to restore the original form of the Vedic hymns, we shall certainly arrive at some kind of Pada text rather than at a Samhitâ text; nay, even in their present form, the original metre and rhythm of the ancient hymns of the Rishis are far more perceptible when the words are divided, than when we join them together throughout according to the rules of Sandhi. Lastly, for practical purposes, the Pada text is far superior to the Samhitâ text in which the final and initial letters, that is, the most important letters of words, are constantly disguised, and liable therefore to different interpretations. Although in some passages we may differ from the interpretation adopted by the Pada text, and although certain Vedic words have, no doubt, been wrongly analysed and divided by Sâkalya, yet such cases are comparatively few, and where they occur, they are interesting as carrying us back to the earliest attempts of Vedic scholarship. In the vast majority of cases the divided text, with a few such rules as we have to observe in reading Latin, nay, even in reading Pâli verses, brings us certainly much nearer to the original utterance of the ancient Rishis than the amalgamated text.

The critical principles by which I have been guided in editing for the first time the text of the Rig-veda, require a few words of explanation, as they have lately been challenged on grounds which, I think, rest on a complete misapprehension of my previous statements on this subject.

As far as we are able to judge at present, we can hardly speak of various readings in the Vedic hymns, in the usual sense of that word. Various readings to be gathered from a collation of different MSS., now accessible to us, there are none. After collating a considerable number of MSS., I have succeeded, I believe, in fixing on three representative MSS., as described in the preface to the first volume of my edition of the Rig-veda. Even these MSS. are not free from blunders,—for what MS. is?—but these blunders have no claim to the title of various readings. They are lapsus calami, and no more; and, what is important, they have not become traditional.

The text, as deduced from the best MSS. of the Samhitâ text, can be controlled by four independent checks. The first is, of course, a collation of the best MSS. of the Samhitâ text.

The second check to be applied to the Samhitâ text is a comparison with the Pada text, of which, again, I possessed at least one excellent MS., and several more modern copies.

The third check was a comparison of this text with Sâyana's commentary, or rather with the text which is presupposed by that commentary. In the few cases where the Pada text seemed to differ from the Samhitâ text, a note was added to that effect, in the various readings of my edition; and the same was done, at least in all important cases, where Sâyana clearly followed a text at variance with our own.

The fourth check was a comparison of any doubtful passage with the numerous passages quoted in the Prâtisâkhya.

These were the principles by which I was guided in the critical restoration of the text of the Rig-veda, and I believe I may say that the text as printed by me is more correct than any MS. now accessible, more trustworthy than the text followed by Sâyana, and in all important points identically the same with that text which the authors of the Prâtisâkhya followed in their critical researches in the fifth or sixth century before our era.

...

Far be it from me to say that the editio princeps of the text thus constituted was printed without mistakes. But most of these mistakes are mistakes which no attentive reader could fail to detect. Cases like II, 35, 1, where *gógi*shat instead of *gó*shishat was printed three times, so as to perplex even Professor Roth, or II, 12, 14, where *sa*samânám occurs three times instead of *sa*samânám, are, I believe, of rare occurrence. Nor do I think that, unless some quite unexpected discoveries are made, there ever will be a new critical edition, or, as we call it in Germany, a new recension of the hymns of the Rig-veda. If by collating new MSS., or by a careful study of the Prâtisâkhya, or by conjectural emendations, a more correct text could have been produced, we may be certain that a critical scholar like Professor Aufrecht would have given us such a text. But after carefully collating several MSS. of Professor Wilson's collection, and after enjoying the advantage of Professor Weber's assistance in collating the MSS. of the Royal Library at Berlin, and after a minute study of the Prâtisâkhya, he frankly states that in the text of the Rig-veda, transcribed in Roman letters, which he printed at Berlin, he followed my edition, and that he had to correct but a small number of misprints. For the two Mandalas which I had not yet published, I lent him the very MSS. on which my edition is founded; and there will be accordingly but few passages in these two concluding Mandalas, which I have still to publish, where the text will materially differ from that of his Romanised transcript.

No one, I should think, who is at all acquainted with the rules of diplomatic criticism, would easily bring himself touch a text resting on such authorities as the text of the Rig-veda. What would a Greek scholar give, if he could say of Homer that his text was in every word, in every syllable, in every vowel, in every accent, the same as the text used by Peisistratos in the sixth century B.C.! A text thus preserved in its integrity for so many centuries, must remain for ever the authoritative text of the Veda.

To remove, for instance, the eleven hymns 49-59 in the eighth Mandala from their proper place, or count them by themselves as Vâlakhilya hymns, seems to me, though no doubt perfectly harmless, little short of a critical sacrilege. Why Sâyana does not explain these hymns, I confess I do not know; but whatever the reason was, it was not because they did not exist at his time, or because he thought them spurious. They are regularly counted in Kâtyâyana's Sarvânukrama, though here the same accident has happened. One commentator, Shadgurusishya, the one most commonly used, does not explain them; but another commentator, Gagannâtha, does explain them, exactly as they occur in the Sarvânukrama, only leaving out hymn 58. That these hymns had something peculiar in the eyes of native scholars, is clear enough. They may for a time have formed a separate collection, they may have been considered of more modern origin. I shall go even further than those who remove these hymns from the place which they have occupied for more than two thousand years. I admit they disturb the regularity both of the Mandala and the Ashtaka divisions, and I have pointed out myself that they are not counted in the ancient Anukramanîs ascribed to Saunaka; (History of Ancient Sanskrit Literature, p. 220.) But, on the other hand, verses taken from these hymns occur in all the other Vedas; they are mentioned by name in the Brâhmanas (Ait. Br. V, 15; VI, 24), the Âranyakas (Ait. Âr. V, 10, p. 445), and the Sûtras (Âsv. Srauta Sûtras, VIII, 2, 3), while they are never included in the manuscripts of Parisishtas or Khilas or apocryphal hymns, nor mentioned by Kâtyâyana as mere Khilas in his Sarvânukrama.

It proves, unless all our views on the chronology of Vedic literature are wrong, that in the fifth century B.C. at least, or previously rather to the time when the Prâtisâkhya was composed, both the Pada and the

Samhitâ texts were so firmly settled that it was impossible, for the sake of uniformity or regularity, to omit one single short a; and it proves à fortiori, that the hymn in which that irregular short a occurs, formed at that time part of the Vedic canon. I confess I feel sometimes frightened by the stringency of this argument, and I should like to see a possibility by which we could explain the addition, not of the Vâlakhilya hymns only, but of other much more modern sounding hymns, at a later time than the period of the Prâtisâkhyas. But until that possibility is shown, we must abide by our own conclusions; and then I ask, who is the critic who would dare to tamper with a canon of scripture of which every iota was settled before the time of Cyrus, and which we possess in exactly that form in which it is described to us by the authors of the Prâtisâkhyas? I say again, that I am not free from misgivings on the subject, and my critical conscience would be far better satisfied if we could ascribe the Prâtisâkhya and all it presupposes to a much later date. But until that is done, the fact remains that the two divergent texts, the Pada and Samhitâ, which we now possess, existed, as we now possess them, previous to the time of the Prâtisâkhya. They have not diverged nor varied since, and the vertex to which they point, starting from the distance of the two texts as measured by the Prâtisâkhya, carries us back far beyond the time of Saunaka, if we wish to determine the date of the first authorised collection of the hymns, both in their Pada and in their Samhitâ form.

...

If these arguments are sound, and if nothing can be said against the critical principles by which I have been guided in editing the text of the Rig-veda, if the fourfold check, described above, fulfils every requirement that could be made for restoring that text which was known to Sâyana, and which was known, probably 2000 years earlier, to the authors of the Prâtisâkhyas, what can be the motives, it may fairly be asked, of those who clamour for a new and more critical edition, and who imagine that the editio princeps of the Rig-veda will share the fate of most of the editiones principes of the Greek and Roman classics, and be supplanted by new editions founded on the collation of other MSS.?

...

It will be seen from these remarks that many things have to be considered before one can form an independent judgment as to the exact view adopted by Sâyana in places where he differs from other authorities, or as to the exact words in which he clothed his meaning. Such cases occur again and again. Thus in IX, 86, I find that Professor Aufrecht ascribes the first ten verses to the Akrishtas, whereas Sâyana calls them Âkrishtas. It is perfectly true that the best MSS. of the Anukramanikâ have Akrishta, it is equally true that the name of these Akrishtas is spelt with a short a in the Harivamsa, 11,533, but an editor of Sâyana's work is not to alter the occasional mistakes of that learned commentator, and Sâyana certainly called these poets Âkrishtas.

Verses 21-30 of the same hymn are ascribed by Professor Aufrecht to the Prisniyah. Here, again, several MSS. support that reading; and in Shadgurusishya's commentary, the correction of prisniyah into prisnayah is made by a later hand. But Sâyana clearly took prisnayah for a nominative plural of prisni, and in this case he certainly was right. The Dictionary of Böhtlingk and Roth quotes the Mahâbhârata, VII, 8728, in support of the peculiar reading of prisniyah, but the published text gives prisnayah. Professor Benfey, in his list of poets (Ind. Stud. vol. iii, p. 223), gives prisniyoga as one word, not prisniyogâ, as stated in the Dictionary of Böhtlingk and Roth, but this is evidently meant for two words, viz. prisnayo[S]gâh. However, whether prisniyah or prisnayah be the real name of these poets, an editor of Sâyana is bound to give that reading of the name which Sâyana believed to be the right one, i. e. prisnayah.

Again, in the same hymn, Professor Aufrecht ascribes verses 31-40 to the Atris. We should then have to read tritîye[S]trayah. But Sâyana read tritîye trayah, and ascribes verses 31-40 to the three companies together of the Rishis mentioned before. On this point the MSS. admit of no doubt, for we read: katurthasya ka dasarkasya âkrishtâ mâshâ ityâdidvinâmânas trayo ganâ drashtârah. I do not say that the other explanation is wrong; I only say that, whether right or wrong, Sâyana certainly read trayah, not atrayah; and an editor of Sâyana has no more right to correct the text, supported by the best MSS., in the first and second, than in the third of these passages, all taken from one and the same hymn.

But though I insist so strongly on a strict observance of the rules of diplomatic criticism with regard to the text of the Rig-veda, nay, even of Sâyana, I insist equally strongly on the right of independent criticism, which ought to begin where diplomatic criticism ends. Considering the startling antiquity which we can claim for every letter and accent of our MSS., so far as they are authenticated by the Prâtisâkhya, to say nothing of the passages of many hymns which are quoted verbatim in the Brâhmanas, the Kalpa-sûtras, the Nirukta, the Brihaddevatâ, and the Anukramanîs, I should deem it reckless to alter one single letter or one single accent in an edition of the hymns of the Rig-veda. As the text has been handed down to us, so it should remain; and whatever alterations and corrections we, the critical Mlekkhas of the nineteenth century, have to propose, should be kept distinct from that time-hallowed inheritance. Unlikely as it may sound, it is true nevertheless that we, the scholars of the nineteenth century, are able to point out mistakes in the text of the Rig-veda which escaped the attention of the most learned among the native scholars of the sixth century B.C. No doubt, these scholars, even if they had perceived such mistakes, would hardly have ventured to correct the text of their sacred writings. The authors of the Prâtisâkhya had before their eyes or ears a text ready made, of which they registered every peculiarity, nay, in which they would note and preserve every single irregularity, even though it stood alone amidst hundreds of analogous cases. With us the case is different. Where we see a rule observed in 99 cases, we feel strongly tempted and sometimes justified in altering the 100th case in accordance with what we consider to be a general rule. Yet even then I feel convinced we ought not to do more than place our conjectural readings below the textus receptus of the Veda,—a text so ancient and venerable that no scholar of any historical tact or critical taste would venture to foist into it a conjectural reading, however plausible, nay, however undeniable.

...

The most powerful instrument that has hitherto been applied to the emendation of Vedic texts, is the metre. Metre means measure, and uniform measure, and hence its importance for critical purposes, as second only to that of grammar. If our knowledge of the metrical system of the Vedic poets rests on a sound basis, any deviations from the general rule are rightly objected to; and if by a slight alteration they can be removed, and the metre be restored, we naturally feel inclined to adopt such emendations. Two safeguards, however, are needed in this kind of conjectural criticism. We ought to be quite certain that the anomaly is impossible, and we ought to be able to explain to a certain extent how the deviation from the original correct text could have occurred. As this subject has of late years received considerable attention, and as emendations of the Vedic texts, supported by metrical arguments, have been carried on a very large scale, it becomes absolutely necessary to reexamine the grounds on which these emendations are supposed to rest. There are, in fact, but few hymns in which some verses or some words have not been challenged for metrical reasons, and I feel bound, therefore, at the very beginning of my translation of the Rig-veda, to express my own opinion on this subject, and to give my reasons why in so many cases I allow metrical anomalies to remain which by some of the most learned and ingenious among Vedic scholars would be pronounced intolerable.

Even if the theory of the ancient metres had not been so carefully worked out by the authors of the Prâtisâkhyas and the Anukramanîs, an independent study of the Veda would have enabled us to discover the general rules by which the Vedic poets were guided in the composition of their works. Nor would it have been difficult to show how constantly these general principles are violated by the introduction of phonetic changes which in the later Sanskrit are called the euphonic changes of Sandhi, and according to which final vowels must be joined with initial vowels, and final consonants adapted to initial consonants, until at last each sentence becomes a continuous chain of closely linked syllables.

It is far easier, as I remarked before, to discover the original and natural rhythm of the Vedic hymns by reading them in the Pada than in the Samhitâ text, and after some practice our ear becomes sufficiently schooled to tell us at once how each line ought to be pronounced. We find, on the one hand, that the rules of Sandhi, instead of being generally binding, were treated by the Vedic poets as poetical licences only; and, on the other, that a greater freedom of pronunciation was allowed even in the body of words than would be tolerated in the later Sanskrit.

But what confirms me even more in my view that such strict uniformity must not be looked for in the ancient hymns of the *Ri*shis, is the fact that in many cases it would he so very easy to replace the irregular by a regular dipodia. Supposing that the original poets had restricted themselves to the dijambus, who could have put in the place of that regular dijambus an irregular dipodia? Certainly not the authors of the Prâtisâkhya, for their ears had clearly discovered the general rhythm of the ancient metres; nor their predecessors, for they had in many instances preserved the tradition of syllables lengthened in accordance with the requirements of the metre. I do not mean to insist too strongly on this argument, or to represent those who handed down the tradition of the Veda as endowed with anything like apaurusheyatva. Strange accidents have happened in the text of the Veda, but they have generally happened when the sense of the hymns had ceased to be understood; and if anything helped to preserve the Veda from greater accidents, it was due, I believe, to the very fact that the metre continued to be understood, and that oral tradition, however much it might fail in other respects, had at all events to satisfy the ears of the hearers. I should have been much less surprised if all irregularities in the metre had been smoothed down by the flux and reflux of oral tradition, a fact which is so apparent in the text of Homer, where the gaps occasioned by the loss of the digamma, were made good by the insertion of unmeaning particles; but I find it difficult to imagine by what class of men, who must have lived between the original poets and the age of the Prâtisâkhyas, the simple rhythm of the Vedic metres should have been disregarded, and the sense of rhythm, which ancient people possess in a far higher degree than we ourselves, been violated through crude and purposeless alterations

...

Wherever we alter the text of the Rig-veda by conjecture, we ought to be able, if possible, to give some explanation how the mistake which we wish to remove came to be committed. If a passage is obscure, difficult to construe, if it contains words which occur in no other place, then we can understand how, during a long process of oral tradition, accidents may have happened. But when everything is smooth and easy, when the intention of the poet is not to be mistaken, when the same phrase has occurred many times before, then to suppose that a simple and perspicuous sentence was changed into a complicated and obscure string of words, is more difficult to understand.

Footnotes

- Since the publication of the first volume of the
  Rig-veda, many new MSS. have come before me,
  partly copied for me, partly lent to me for a time
  by scholars in India, but every one of them
  belonged clearly to one of the three families
  which I have described in my introduction to the
  first volume of the Rig-veda. In the beginning of
  the first Ash*t*aka, and occasionally at the
  beginning of other Ash*t*akas, likewise in the
  commentary on hymns which were studied by
  native scholars with particular interest, various
  readings occur in some MSS., which seem at
  first to betoken an independent source, but
  which are in reality mere marginal notes, due to
  more or less learned students of these MSS.
  Thus after verse 3 of the introduction one MS.
  reads: sa prâha n*ri*pati*m*, râ*g*an, sâya*n*âryo
  mamânu*gah*, sarva*m* vetty esha vedânâ*m*
  vyâkhyâtr*i*tvena, yu*g*yatâm. The same MS., after
  verse 4, adds: ityukto mâdhavârye*n*a
  vîrabukkamahîpati*h*, anva*s*ât sâyâ*n*âkâryam
  vedârthasya prakâ*s*ane.
- I had for a time some hope that MSS. written in
  Grantha or other South-Indian alphabets might
  have preserved an independent text of Sâya*n*a,
  but from some specimens of a Grantha MS.
  collated for me by Mr. Eggeling, I do not think
  that even this hope is meant to be realised. The
  MS. in question contains a few independent
  various readings, such as are found in all MSS.,
  and owe their origin clearly to the jottings of

individual students. when at the end of verse 6, I found the independent reading, vyutpannas tâvatâ sarvâ *riko* vyâkhyâtum arhati, I expected that other various readings of the same character might follow.

- A number of various readings which have been gleaned from Pandit Târânâtha's Tulâdânâdipaddhati (see Trübner's American and Oriental Literary Record, July 31, 1868) belong to the same class. They may be due either to the copyists of the MSS. which Pandit Târânâtha used while compiling his work, or they may by accident have crept into his own MS. Anyhow, not one of them is supported either by the best MSS. accessible in Europe, or by any passage in the Prâtisâkhya.

II

HYMNS OF THE SAMAVEDA

Translated with a Popular Commentary

Ralph T.H. Griffith

1895

PREFACE

The Collection is made up of hymns, portions of hymns, and detached verses, taken mainly from the *Rgveda*, transposed and re-arranged, without reference to their original order, to suit the religious ceremonies in which they were to be employed. In these compiled hymns there are frequent variations, of more or less importance, from the text of the *Rgveda* as we now possess it which variations, although in some cases they are apparently explanatory, seem in others to be older and more original than the readings of the *Rgveda*. In singing, the verses are still further altered by prolongation, repetition and insertion of syllables, and various modulations, rests, and other modifications prescribed, for the guidance of the officiating priests, in the Ganas or Song-books. Two of these manuals, the Gramageyagdna, or Congregational, and the Aranyagana or Forest Song-Book, follow the order of the verses of part I, of the Sanhita, and two others, the Uhagana, the Uhyagana, of Part II. This part is less disjointed than part I, and is generally arranged in triplets whose first verse is often the repetition of a verse that has occurred in part I.

...

There are three recensions of the text of the *Samaveda Sanhita*, the Kauthuma Sakha or recension is current in Guzerat, the Jaiminiya in the Carnatic, and the Ranayaniya in the Mahratta country. A translation, by Dr. Stevenson, of the Ranayaniya recension - or, rather, a free version of Sayana's paraphrase-was edited by Professor Wilson, in 1842; in 1848 Professor Benfey of Göttingen brought out an excellent edition of the same text with a metrical translation, a complete glossary, and explanatory notes; and in 1874-78 Pandit Satyavrata Samasrami of Calcutta published in the Bibliotheca Indicaa a most meritorious edition of the Sanhita according to the same recension, with Sayana's commentary, portions of the Song-books, and in other illustrative matter. I have followed Benfey's text, and have, made much use of his glossary and notes. Pandit Satyavrata Samasrami's edition also has been of the greatest service to me. To Mr. Venis, Principal of the Benares Sanskrit College, I am indebted for, the loan of the College manuscripts of the text and commentary.

III

THE

SÁNKHYA APHORISMS

OF

KAPILA,

WITH

Illustrative Extracts from the Commentaries.

TRANSLATED BY

JAMES R. BALLANTYNE, LL. D.,

LATE PRINCIPAL OF THE BENARES COLLEGE.

THIRD EDITION.

LONDON:
TRÜBNER & CO., LUDGATE HILL.
1885.

ADVERTISEMENT.

THE present work, both in its Sanskrit portion and in its English, is an amended reprint of three volumes(1), published in India, which have already become very scarce. An abridged form of those volumes(2), which subsequently appeared, contains nothing of the Sanskrit original but the Aphorisms.

While, in the following pages, all the corrections obtainable from the abridgment have been turned to account, an immense number of improved readings have been taken from another source. Three several times I carefully read Dr. Ballantyne's translation in as many different copies of it; entering suggestions, in the second copy, without reference to those which had been entered in the first, and similarly making independent suggestions in my third copy. All these (3) were, on various occasions, submitted to Dr. Ballantyne; and such of them as did not meet his approval were crossed through. The residue, many more than a thousand, have been embodied in the ensuing sheets, but are not indicated(4), as successively introduced. The renderings proposed in the footnotes are, for the most part, from among those which have recently occurred to me as eligible.

That Dr. Ballantyne had any thought of reissuing, in whatever form, the volumes mentioned at the beginning of this Advertisement, I was unaware, till some years after he had made over the abridgment of

them to Professor Cowell, for publication. (5)
Otherwise, I should have placed at his disposal the
materials towards improvement of his second edition,
which, at the cost of no slight drudgery, are here made
available.

The Sánkhya Aphorisms, in all the known
commentaries on them, are exhibited word for word.
The variants, now given, of the Aphorisms, afforded by
accessible productions of that character, have been
drawn from the works, of which only one has yet been
printed, about to be specified: (6)

I. The *Sánkhya-pravachana-bháshya*, by Vijnána
Bhikshu. Relevant particulars I have given elsewhere.
My oldest MS. of it was transcribed in 1654.

II. The *Kápila-sánkhya-pravachana-sútra-vṛitti*, by
Aniruddha. Of this I have consulted, besides a MS.
copied in 1818, formerly the property of Dr.
Ballantyne, one which I procured to be copied, in
1855, from an old MS. without date.

III. The *Laghhu-sánkhya-sútra-vṛitti*, by Nagesa. Of this
I have two MSS., both undated. One of them is entire;
but the other is defective by the three first Books.

IV. The *Sánkhya-pravachana-sútra-vṛitti-sára*, by
Vedánti Mahádeva. Here, again, only one of two MSS.
which I possess is complete. The other, which breaks
off in the midst of the comment on Book II., Aph. 15,
is, in places, freely interpolated from No. I. Neither of
them has a date.

Nearly all my longer annotations, and some of the shorter, were scrutinized, while in the rough, by the learned Professor Cowell, but for whose searching criticisms, which cannot be valued too highly, they would, in several instances, have been far less accurate than they now are.

F. H.

MARLESFORD, SUFFOLK,
Aug. 28, 1884.

Footnotes

1. Their titles here follow:

"The Aphorisms of the Sánkhya Philosophy of Kapila, with Illustrative Extracts from the Commentaries. [Book I.] Printed for the use of the Benares College, by order of Govt. N. W. P. Allahabad: Printed at the Presbyterian Mission Press. Rev. L. G. HAY, *Sup't.* 1852."

"The Aphorisms of the Sánkhya Philosophy, by Kapila, with Illustrative Extracts from the Commentary. Books II., III., & IV. In Sanskrit and English, Printed for the use of the Benares College, by order of Govt. N. W. P. (1st Edition, 550 *Copies:— Price* 12 *annas.*) Allahabad: Printed at the Presbyterian Mission Press. Rev. L. G. HAY, *Superintendent.* 1854."

"The Aphorisms of the Sánkhya Philosophy, by Kapila, with Illustrative Extracts from the Commentary by Vijnána-Bhikshu. Books V. & VI. Sanskrit and English. Translated by James R. Ballantyne, LL.D., Principal of the Govt. College, Benares. Printed for the use of the Benares College, by order of Govt. N. W. P . (1st Edition, 550 *Copies*:—Price 12 *annas.*) Allahabad: Printed at the Presbyterian Mission Press. Rev. L. G. HAY, *Sup't.* 1856."

2. Occupying Fasciculi 32 and 81 of the New Series of the *Bibliotheca Indica*, issued in 1862 and 1865. The proof-sheets of only 32 pages of the whole, from the beginning, were read by Dr. Ballantyne; the rest, by Professor Cowell.

The title of the abridged form runs: "The Sánkhya Aphorisms of Kapila, with Extracts from Vijnána Bhiks[h]u's Commentary," &c. But this is a misrepresentation, as regards Book I., which takes up 63 pages out of the total of 175. The expository matter in that Book is derived, very largely, from other commentators than Vijnána. Vedánti Mahádeva mainly supplies it at the outset, and, towards the end, well nigh exclusively, Aniruddha. Some share of it, however, will not be traced; it having been furnished by one of Dr. Ballantyne's pandits, whom I have repeatedly seen in the very act, as by his own acknowledgment, of preparing his elucidations.

3. Many of them, especially in Books II.-VI., rest on readings of the original preferable to those which had been accepted.

Though not fully published till 1856, my edition of the *Sánkkya-pravachana-bhảshya*, its preface alone excepted, was in print as early as 1853; and Dr. Ballantyne had a copy of it. A few arbitrarily chosen words apart, his text, after Book I., is borrowed from it throughout, but with no mention of the fact. My advice was unheeded, that he should profit by the copious emendations which I had amassed and digested from better manuscripts than those to which I at first had access. Greatly to his disservice, he would not be induced even to look at them. It faring the same with my typographical corrections, he has, here and there, reproduced errors, more or less gross, which might easily have been avoided. See, for specimens. pp. 197, 288, 357, 373, 374, 381, 390.

4. Nor has attention been topically directed to sundry blemishes of idiom which have been removed; as, for example, by the substitution of 'unless' for 'without,' of 'in time' for 'through time,' of 'presently' for 'just,' and of 'between the two' for 'between both.'

5. "At the time of his departure from India, in 1860, Dr. Ballantyne left with me the MS. of his revised translation of the Sánkhya Aphorisms," "Notice," in the Bibliotheca Indica, New Series, No, 81.

6. For details respecting these commentaries and their authors, see my *Contribution towards an Index to the*

Bibliography of the Indian Philosophical Systems, or my Preface to the *Sánkhya-sára.*

I once had a second copy of this very rare work, bearing no date, but most venerable in appearance. Like many of my manuscript treasures, it was lent, and never found its way back to me.

IV

The

Sacred Books of the East

Translated

By various Oriental scholars

and edited by

F. Max Müller

Vol. I

The Upanishads

Translated by F. Max Müller

In two parts

Part I

Oxford, the Clarendon Press

[1879]

TO

THE RIGHT HONOURABLE THE MARQUIS OF SALISBURY, K*G*.

CHANCELLOR OF THE UNIVERSITY OF OXFORD,

LATELY SECRETARY OF STATE FOR INDIA,

SIR HENRY J. S. MAINE, K.O*S*.I.

MEMBER OF THE COUNCIL OF INDIA,

AND

THE VERY REV. H. G. LIDDELL, D*D*.

DEAN OF CHRIST CHURCH,

TO WHOSE KIND INTEREST AND EXERTIONS

THIS ATTEMPT TO MAKE KNOWN TO THE ENGLISH PEOPLE

THE SACRED BOOKS OF THE EAST

IS SO LARGELY INDEBTED,

I NOW DEDICATE THESE VOLUMES WITH SINCERE RESPECT AND GRATITUDE,

F. MAX MÜLLER.

PREFACE

TO

THE SACRED BOOKS OF THE EAST

Most of the ancient sacred books have been handed down by oral tradition for many generations before they were consigned to writing....

Hence, what had been said by these half-human, half-divine ancestors, if it was preserved at all, was soon looked upon as a more than human utterance. It was received with reverence, it was never questioned and criticised.

Some of these ancient sayings were preserved because they were so true and so striking that they could not be forgotten. They contained eternal truths, expressed for the first time in human language

Nor must we forget that though oral tradition, when once brought under proper discipline, is a most faithful guardian, it is not without its dangers in its incipient stages. Many a word may have been misunderstood, many a sentence confused, as it was told by father to son, before it became fixed in the tradition of a village community, and then resisted by its very sacredness all attempts at emendation.

Lastly, we must remember that those who handed down the ancestral treasures of ancient wisdom, would often feel inclined to add what seemed useful to themselves, and what they knew could be preserved in one way only, namely, if it was allowed to form part of the tradition that had to be handed down, as a sacred trust, from generation to generation. The priestly influence was at work, even before there were priests by profession, and when the priesthood had once become professional, its influence may account for much that would otherwise seem inexplicable in the sacred codes of the ancient world.

PROGRAM OF A TRANSLATION

OF

THE SACRED BOOKS OF THE EAST.

I here subjoin the program in which I first put forward the idea of a translation of the Sacred Books of the East, and through which I invited the co-operation of Oriental scholars in this undertaking. The difficulty of finding translators, both willing and competent to take a part in it, proved far greater than I had anticipated. Even when I had secured the assistance of a number of excellent scholars, and had received their promises of prompt co-operation, illness, domestic affliction, and even death asserted their control over all human affairs. Professor Childers, who had shown the warmest interest in our work, and on whom I chiefly depended for the Pali literature of the Buddhists, was taken from us, an irreparable loss to Oriental scholarship in general, and to our undertaking in particular. Among native scholars, whose co-operation I had been particularly desired to secure, Rajendralal Mitra, who had promised a translation of the Vâyu-purâna, was prevented by serious illness from fulfilling his engagement. In other cases sorrow and sickness have caused, at all events, serious delay in the translation of the very books which were to have inaugurated this Series. However, new offers of assistance have come, and I hope that more may still come from Oriental scholars both in India and England, so that the limit of time which had been originally assigned to the publication of twenty-four volumes may not, I hope, be much exceeded.

THE SACRED BOOKS OF THE EAST, TRANSLATED, WITH INTRODUCTIONS AND NOTES, BY VARIOUS ORIENTAL SCHOLARS, AND EDITED BY F. MAX MULLER.

Apart from the interest which the Sacred Books of all religions possess in the eyes of the theologian, and, more particularly, of the missionary, to whom an accurate knowledge of them is as indispensable as a knowledge of the enemy's country is to a general, these works have of late assumed a new importance, as viewed in the character of ancient historical documents. In every country where Sacred Books have been preserved, whether by oral tradition or by writing, they are the oldest records, and mark the beginning of what may be called documentary, in opposition to purely traditional, history.

...

This being the case, it was but natural that the attention of the historian should of late have been more strongly attracted by these Sacred Books, as likely to afford most valuable information, not only on the religion, but also on the moral sentiments, the social institutions, the legal maxims of some of the most important nations of antiquity. There are not many nations that have preserved sacred writings, and many of those that have been preserved have but lately become accessible to us in their original form, through the rapid advance of Oriental scholarship in Europe. Neither Greeks, nor Romans, nor Germans, nor Celts, nor Slaves have left us anything that deserves the name of Sacred Books....

Oriental scholars have been blamed for not having as yet supplied a want so generally felt, and so frequently expressed, as a complete, trustworthy, and readable translation of the principal Sacred Books of the Eastern Religions. The reasons, however, why hitherto they have shrunk from such an undertaking are clear enough. The difficulties in many cases of giving complete translations, and not selections only, are very great. There is still much work to be done in a critical restoration of the original texts, in an examination of their grammar and metres, and in determining the exact meaning of many words and passages. That kind of work is naturally far more attractive to scholars than a mere translation, particularly when they cannot but feel that, with the progress of our knowledge, many a passage which now seems clear and easy, may, on being re-examined, assume a new import. Thus while scholars who are most competent to undertake a translation, prefer to devote their time to more special researches, the work of a complete translation is deferred to the future, and historians are left under the impression that Oriental scholarship is still in so unsatisfactory a state as to make any reliance on translations of the Veda, the Avesta, or the Tâo-te King extremely hazardous.

It is clear, therefore, that a translation of the principal Sacred Books of the East can be carried out only at a certain sacrifice. Scholars must leave for a time their own special researches in order to render the general results already obtained accessible to the public at large. And even then, really useful results can be achieved viribus unitis only. If four of the best Egyptologists have to combine in order to produce a satisfactory edition and translation of one of the Sacred Books of ancient Egypt, a much larger number of Oriental scholars will be required for translating the Sacred Books of the Brahmans, the Buddhists, the Zoroastrians, the followers of Khung-fû-ʒze, Lâo-ʒze, and Mohammed.

Lastly, there was the most serious difficulty of all, a difficulty which no scholar could remove, viz. the difficulty of finding the funds necessary for carrying out so large an undertaking. No doubt there exists at present a very keen interest in questions connected with the origin, the growth, and decay of religion. But much of that interest is theoretic rather than historical. How people might or could or should have elaborated religious ideas, is a topic most warmly discussed among psychologists and theologians, but a study of the documents, in which alone the actual growth of religious thought can be traced, is much neglected.

...

Having been so fortunate as to secure that support, having also received promises of assistance from some

of the best Oriental scholars in England and India, I
hope I shall be able, after the necessary preparations
are completed, to publish about three volumes of
translations every year, selecting from the stores of the
six so-called 'Book-religions' those works which at
present can be translated, and which are most likely to
prove useful. All translations will be made from the
original texts, and where good translations exist
already, they will be carefully revised by competent
scholars. Such is the bulk of the religious literature of
the Brahmans and the Buddhists, that to attempt a
complete translation would be far beyond the powers
of one generation of scholars. Still, if the interest in the
work itself should continue, there is no reason why
this series of translations should not be carried on,
even after those who commenced it shall have ceased
from their labours.

What I contemplate at present and I am afraid at my
time of life even this may seem too sanguine, is no
more than a Series of twenty-four volumes, the
publication of which will probably extend over eight
years.

POSITION OF THE UPANISHADS IN VEDIC LITERATURE.

My real love for Sanskrit literature was first kindled by the Upanishads. It was in the year 1844, when attending Schelling's lectures at Berlin, that my attention was drawn to those ancient theosophic treatises, and I still possess my collations of the Sanskrit MSS. which had then just arrived at Berlin, the Chambers collection, and my copies of commentaries, and commentaries on commentaries, which I made at that time. Some of my translations which I left with Schelling, I have never been able to recover, though to judge from others which I still possess, the loss of them is of small consequence. Soon after leaving Berlin, when continuing my Sanskrit studies at Paris under Burnouf, I put aside the Upanishads, convinced that for a true appreciation of them it was necessary to study, first of all, the earlier periods of Vedic literature, as represented by the hymns and the Brâhmaṇas of the Vedas.

In returning, after more than thirty years, to these favourite studies, I find that my interest in them, though it has changed in character, has by no means diminished.

It is true, no doubt, that the stratum of literature which contains the Upanishads is later than the Samhitâs, and later than the Brâhmaṇas, but the first germs of Upanishad doctrines go back at least as far as the Mantra period, which provisionally has been fixed between 1000 and 800 B.C. Conceptions corresponding to the general teaching of the Upanishads occur in certain hymns of the Rig-veda-samhitâ, they must have existed therefore before that collection was finally closed. One hymn in the Samhitâ of the Rig-veda (I, 191) was designated by Kâtyâyana, the author of the Sarvânukramanikâ, as an Upanishad. Here, however, upanishad means rather a secret charm than a philosophical doctrine. Verses of the hymns have often been incorporated in the Upanishads, and among the Oupnekhats translated into Persian by Dârâ Shukoh we actually find the Purusha-sûkta, the 90th hymn of the tenth book of the Rig-veda, forming the greater portion of the Bark'heh Soukt. In the Samhitâ of the Yagur-veda, however, in the Vâgasaneyisâkhâ, we meet with a real Upanishad, the famous Îsâ or Îsâvâsya-upanishad, while the Sivasamkalpa, too, forms part of its thirty-fourth book. In the Brâhmanas several Upanishads occur, even in portions which are not classed as Âranyakas, as, for instance, the well-known Kena or Talavakâra upanishad. The recognised place, however, for the ancient Upanishads is in the Âranyakas, or forest-books, which, as a rule, form an appendix to the Brâhmanas, but are sometimes included also under the general name of Brâhmana. Brâhmana, in fact, meaning originally the sayings of Brahmans, whether in the general sense of priests, or in the more special of Brahman-priest, is a name applicable not only to the books, properly so called, but to all old prose traditions, whether contained in the Samhitâs, such as the Taittirîya-samhitâ, the Brâhmanas, the Âranyakas, the Upanishads, and even, in certain cases, in the Sûtras. We shall see in the introduction to the Aitareya-âranyaka, that that Âranyaka is in the beginning a Brâhmana, a mere continuation of the Aitareya-brâhmana, explaining the Mahâvrata ceremony, while its last book contains the Sûtras or short technical rules explaining the same ceremony which in the first book had been treated in the style peculiar to the Brâhmanas. In the same Aitareya-âranyaka, III, 2, 6, 6, a passage of the Upanishad is spoken of as a Brâhmana, possibly as something like a Brâhmana, while something very like an Upanishad occurs in the Âpastamba-sûtras, and might be quoted therefore as a Sûtra. At all events the Upanishads, like the Âranyakas, belong to what Hindu theologians call Sruti, or revealed literature, in opposition to Smriti, or traditional literature, which is supposed to be founded on the former, and allowed to claim a secondary authority only; and the earliest of these philosophical treatises will always, I believe, maintain a place in the literature of the world, among the most astounding productions of the human mind in any age and in any country.

DIFFERENT CLASSES OF UPANISHADS.

The ancient Upanishads, i. e. those which occupy a place in the Samhitâs, Brâhmanas, and Âranyakas, must be, if we follow the chronology which at present is commonly, though, it may be, provisionally only, received by Sanskrit scholars, older than 600 B.C., i.e. anterior to the rise of Buddhism (1). As to other Upanishads, and their number is very large, which either stand by themselves, or which are ascribed to the Atharva-veda, it is extremely difficult to fix their age. Some of them are, no doubt, quite modern, for mention is made even of an Allah-upanishad; but others may claim a far higher antiquity than is generally assigned to them on internal evidence. I shall only mention that the name of Atharvasiras, an Upanishad generally assigned to a very modern date, is quoted in the Sûtras of Gautama and Baudhâyana; that the Svetâsvatara-upanishad, or the Svetâsvataranâm Mantropanishad, though bearing many notes of later periods of thought, is quoted by Sankara in his commentary on the Vedânta-sûtras; while the Nrisimhottaratâpanîya-upanishad forms part of the twelve Upanishads explained by Vidyâranya in his Sarvopanishad-arthânubhûti-prakâsa. The Upanishads comprehended in that work are:

1. Aitareya-upanishad.
2. Taittirîya-upanishad.
3. *Kh*ândogya-upanishad.
4. Mu*nd*aka-upanishad.
5. Prasna-upanishad.
6. Kaushîtaki-upanishad.
7. Maitrâya*n*îya-upanishad.
8. Ka*th*avallî-upanishad.
9. *S*vetâ*s*vatara-upanishad.
10. Br*ih*ad-âra*n*yaka-upanishad.
11. Talavakâra (Kena)-upanishad.
12. N*risim*hottaratâpanîya-upanishad (2)

The number of Upanishads translated by Dârâ Shukoh amounts to 50; their number, as given in the Mahâvâkyamuktâvalî and in the Muktikâ-upanishad, is 108. Professor Weber thinks that their number, so far as we know at present, may be reckoned at 235. In order, however, to arrive at so high a number, every title of an Upanishad would have to be counted separately, while in several cases it is clearly the same Upanishad which is quoted under different names. In an alphabetical list which I published in 1855 (Zeitschrift der Deutschen Morgenländischen Gesellschaft XIX, 137-158), the number of real Upanishads reached 149. To that number Dr. Burnell in his Catalogue (p. 59) added 5, Professor Haug (Brahma und die Brahmanen) 16, making a sum total of 170. New names, however, are constantly being added in the catalogues of MSS. published by Bühler, Kielhorn, Burnell, Rajendralal Mitra, and others, and I shall reserve therefore a more complete list of Upanishads for a later volume (3).

Though it is easy to see that these Upanishads belong
to very different periods of Indian thought, any attempt
to fix their relative age seems to me for the present
almost hopeless. No one can doubt that the
Upanishads which have had a place assigned to them
in the Samhitâs, Brâhmanas, and Âranyakas are the
oldest. Next to these we can draw a line to include the
Upanishads clearly referred to in the Vedânta-sûtras,
or explained and quoted by Sankara, by Sâyana, and
other more modern commentators. We can distinguish
Upanishads in prose from Upanishads in mixed prose
and verse, and again Upanishads in archaic verse from
Upanishads in regular and continuous Anushtubh
Slokas. We can also class them according to their
subjects, and, at last, according to the sects to which
they belong. But beyond this it is hardly safe to
venture at present. Attempts have been made by
Professor Weber and M. Regnaud to fix in each class
the relative age of certain Upanishads, and I do not
deny to their arguments, even where they conflict with
each other, considerable weight in forming a
preliminary judgment. But I know of hardly any
argument which is really convincing, or which could
not be met by counter arguments equally strong.
Simplicity may be a sign of antiquity, but it is not so
always, for what seems simple, may be the result of
abbreviation. One Upanishad may give the correct,
another an evidently corrupt reading, yet it does not
follow that the correct reading may not be the result of
an emendation. It is quite clear that a large mass of
traditional Upanishads must have existed before they
assumed their present form. Where two or three or
four Upanishads contain the same story, told almost

in the same words, they are not always copied from one another, but they have been settled independently, in different localities, by different teachers, it may be, for different purposes. Lastly, the influence of Sâkhâs or schools may have told more or less on certain Upanishads. Thus the Maitrâyanîya-upanishad, as we now possess it, shows a number of irregular forms which even the commentator can account for only as peculiarities of the Maitrâyanîya-sâkhâ. That Upanishad, as it has come down to us, is full of what we should call clear indications of a modern and corrupt age. It contains in VI, 37, a sloka from the Mânava-dharma-sâstra, which startled even the commentator, but is explained away by him as possibly found in another Sâkhâ, and borrowed from there by Manu. It contains corruptions of easy words which one would have thought must have been familiar to every student. Thus instead of the passage as found in the Khândogya-upanishad VIII, 7, 1, ya âtmâpahatapâpmâ vigaro vimrityur visoko 'vigighatso 'pipâsah, &c., the text of the Maitrâyanîya-upanishad (VII, 7) reads, âtmâpahatapâpmâ vigaro vimrityur visoko 'vikikitso 'vipâsah. But here again the commentator explains that another Sâkhâ reads 'vigighatsa, and that avipâsa is to be explained by means of a change of letters as apipâsa. Corruptions, therefore, or modern elements which are found in one Upanishad, as handed down in one Sâkhâ, do not prove that the same existed in other Sâkhâs, or that they were found in the original text (4).

All these questions have to be taken into account before we can venture to give a final judgment on the relative age of Upanishads which belong to one and the same class. I know of no problem which offers so many similarities with the one before us as that of the relative age of the four Gospels. All the difficulties which occur in the Upanishads occur here, and no critical student who knows the difficulties that have to be encountered in determining the relative age of the four Gospels, will feel inclined, in the present state of Vedic scholarship, to speak with confidence on the relative age of the ancient Upanishads.

Footnotes

1. Gautama, translated by Bühler, Sacred Books of the East, vol. ii, p. 272, and Introduction, p. lvi.
2. One misses the Îsâ or Îsâvâsya-upanishad in this list. The Upanishads chiefly studied in Bengal are the Brĭhad-âranyaka, Aitareya, Khândogya, Taittirîya, Îsâ, Kena, Katha, Prasna, Mundaka, and Mândûkya, to which should be added the Svetâsvatara. MM., History of Ancient Sanskrit Literature, p. 325.
3. Dr. Burnell thinks that this is an artificial computation, 108 being a sacred number in Southern India. See Kielhorn in Gough's Papers on Ancient Sanskrit Literature, p. 193.
4. They are generally explained as khândasa, but in one place (Maitr. Up. II, 4) the commentator treats such irregularities as etakkhâkhâsanketapâthah, a reading peculiar to the Maitrâyanîya school. Some learned remarks

on this point may be seen in an article by Dr. L.
Schroeder, Über die Maitrâyanî Samhitâ.

CRITICAL TREATMENT OF THE TEXT OF THE UPANISHADS.

With regard to a critical restoration of the text of the Upanishads, I have but seldom relied on the authority of new MSS., but have endeavoured throughout to follow that text which is presupposed by the commentaries, whether they are the work of the old Sankarâkârya, or of the more modern Sankarânanda, or Sâyana, or others. Though there still prevails some uncertainty as to the date of Sankarâkârya, commonly assigned to the eighth century A.D., yet I doubt whether any MSS. of the Upanishads could now be found prior to 1000 A.D. The text, therefore, which Sankara had before his eyes, or, it may be, his ears, commands, I think, a higher authority than that of any MSS. likely to be recovered at present.

It may be objected that Sankara's text belonged to one locality only, and that different readings and different recensions may have existed in other parts of India. That is perfectly true. We possess various recensions of several Upanishads, as handed down in different Sâkhâs of different Vedas, and we know of various readings recorded by the commentators. These, where they are of importance for our purposes, have been carefully taken into account.

It has also been supposed that Sankara, who, in writing his commentaries on the Upanishad, was chiefly guided by philosophical considerations, his chief object being to use the Upanishads as a sacred foundation for the Vedânta philosophy, may now and then have taken liberties with the text. That may be so, but no stringent proof of it has as yet been brought forward, and I therefore hold that when we succeed in establishing throughout that text which served as the basis of Saṅkara's commentaries, we have done enough for the present, and have fulfilled at all events the first and indispensable task in a critical treatment of the text of the Upanishads.

But in the same manner as it is easy to see that the text of the Rig-veda, which is presupposed by Sâyana's commentary and even by earlier works, is in many places palpably corrupt, we cannot resist the same conviction with regard to the text of the Upanishads. In some cases the metre, in others grammar, in others again the collation of analogous passages enable us to detect errors, and probably very ancient errors, that had crept into the text long before Saṅkara composed his commentaries.

Some questions connected with the metres of the Upanishads have been very learnedly treated by Professor Gildemeister in his essay, 'Zur Theorie des Sloka.' The lesson to be derived from that essay, and from a study of the Upanishads, is certainly to abstain for the present from conjectural emendations. In the old Upanishads the same metrical freedom prevails as in the hymns; in the later Upanishads, much may be tolerated as the result of conscious or unconscious imitation. The metrical emendations that suggest themselves are generally so easy and so obvious that, for that very reason, we should hesitate before correcting what native scholars would have corrected long ago, if they had thought that there was any real necessity for correction.

It is easy to suggest, for instance, that in the Vâgasaneyi-samhitâ-upanishad, verse 5, instead of tad antar asya sarvasya, tadu sarvasyâsya bâhyatah, the original text may have been tad antar asya sarvasya tadu sarvasya bâhyatah; yet Sankara evidently read sarvasyâsya, and as the same reading is found in the text of the Vâgasaneyi-samhitâ, who would venture to correct so old a mistake?

Again, if in verse 8, we left out yâthâtathyatah, we should get a much more regular metre,

Kavir manîshî paribhûh svyambhûh
arthân vyadahâk khâsvatîbhyai samâbhyah.

Here vyada forms one syllable by what I have proposed to call synizesis, which is allowed in the Upanishads as well as in the hymns. All would then seem right, except that it is difficult to explain how so rare a word as yâthâtathyatah could have been introduced into the text.

In verse 10 one feels tempted to propose the omission of eva in anyad âhur avidyayâ, while in verse 11, an eva inserted after vidyâm ka would certainly improve the metre.

In verse 15 the expression satyadharmâya drishtaye is archaic, but perfectly legitimate in the sense of 'that we may see the nature of the True,' or 'that we see him whose nature is true.' When this verse is repeated in the Maitr. Up. VI, 35, we find instead, satyadharmâya vishnave, 'for the true Vishnu.' But here, again, no sound critic would venture to correct a mistake, intentional or unintentional, which is sanctioned both by the MSS. of the text and by the commentary.

Such instances, where every reader feels tempted at once to correct the textus receptus, occur again and again, and when they seem of any interest they have been mentioned in the notes. It may happen, however, that the correction, though at first sight plausible, has to be surrendered on more mature consideration. Thus in the Vâgasaneyi-samhitâ-upanishad, verse 2, one feels certainly inclined to write evam tve nânyatheto 'sti, instead of evam tvayi nânyatheto 'sti. But tve, if it were used here, would probably itself have to be pronounced dissyllabically, while tvayi, though it never occurs in the Rig-veda, may well keep its place here, in the last book of the Vâgasaneyi-samhitâ, provided we pronounce it by synizesis, i. e. as one syllable.

Attempts have been made sometimes to go beyond Sankara, and to restore the text, as it ought to have been originally, but as it was no longer in Sankara's time. It is one thing to decline to follow Sankara in every one of his interpretations, it is quite another to decline to accept the text which he interprets. The former is inevitable, the latter is always very precarious.

Thus I see, for instance, that M. Regnaud, in the Errata to the second volume of his excellent work on the Upanishads (Matériaux pour servir à l'histoire de la philosophie de l'Inde, 1878) proposes to read in the Brihad-âranyaka upanishad IV, 3, 1-8, sam anena vadishya iti, instead of sa mene na vadishya iti. Sankara adopted the latter reading, and explained accordingly, that Yâgñavalkya went to king Ganaka, but made up his mind not to speak. M. Regnaud, reading sam anena vadishya iti, takes the very opposite view, namely, that Yâgñavalkya went to king Ganaka, having made up his mind to have a conversation with him. As M. Regnaud does not rest this emendation on the authority of any new MSS., we may examine it as an ingenious conjecture; but in that case it seems to me clear that, if we adopted it, we should have at the same time to omit the whole sentence which follows. Sankara saw clearly that what had to be accounted or explained was why the king should address the Brahman first, samrâd eva pûrvam paprakkha; whereas if Yâgñavalkya had come with the intention of having a conversation with the king, he, the Brahman, should have spoken first. This irregularity is explained by the intervening sentence, in which we are reminded that on a former occasion, when Ganaka and Yâgñavalkya had a disputation on the Agnihotra, Yâgñavalkya granted Ganaka a boon to choose, and he chose as his boon the right of asking questions according to his pleasure. Having received that boon, Ganaka was at liberty to question Yâgñavalkya, even though he did not like it, and hence Ganaka is introduced here as the first to ask a question.

All this hangs well together, while if we assume that Yâgñavalkya came for the purpose of having a conversation with Ganaka, the whole sentence from 'atha ha yag ganakas ka' to 'pûrvam paprakkha' would be useless, nor would there be any excuse for Ganaka beginning the conversation, when Yâgñavalkya came himself on purpose to question him.

It is necessary, even when we feel obliged to reject an interpretation of Sankara's, without at the same time altering the text, to remember that Sankara, where he is not blinded by philosophical predilections, commands the highest respect as an interpreter. I cannot help thinking therefore that M. Regnaud (vol. i, p. 59) was right in translating the passage in the Khând. Up. V, 3, 7, tasmâd usarveshu lokeshu kshattrasyaiva prasâsanam abhût, by 'que le kshatriya seul l'a enseignée dans tous les mondes.' For when he proposes in the 'Errata' to translate instead, 'ç'est pourquoi l'empire dans tous les mondes fut attribué au kshatriya seulement,' he forgets that such an idea is foreign to the ordinary atmosphere in which the Upanishads move. It is not on account of the philosophical knowledge possessed by a few Kshatriyas, such as Ganaka or Pravâhana, that the privilege of government belongs everywhere to the second class. That rests on a totally different basis. Such exceptional knowledge, as is displayed by a few kings, might be an excuse for their claiming the privileges belonging to the Brahmans, but it would never, in the eyes of the ancient Indian Âryas, be considered as an argument for their claiming kingly power. Therefore, although I am well aware that prasâs is most frequently used in the sense of ruling, I have no doubt that Sankara likewise was fully aware of that, and that if he nevertheless explained prasâsana here in the sense of prasâstrĭtvam sishyânâm, he did so because this meaning too was admissible, particularly here, where we may actually translate it by proclaiming, while the other meaning, that of ruling, would simply be impossible in the concatenation of ideas, which is placed before us in the Upanishad.

It seems, no doubt, extremely strange that neither the last redactors of the text of the Upanishads, nor the commentators, who probably knew the principal Upanishads by heart, should have perceived how certain passages in one Upanishad represented the same or nearly the same text which is found in another Upanishad, only occasionally with the most palpable corruptions.

Thus when the ceremony of offering a mantha or mash is described, we read in the Khândogya-upanishad V, 2, 6, that it is to be accompanied by certain words which on the whole are intelligible. But when the same passage occurs again in the Brĭhad-âranyaka, those words have been changed to such a degree, and in two different ways in the two Sâkhâs of the Mâdhyandinas and Kânvas, that, though the commentator explains them, they are almost unintelligible.

I shall place the three passages together in three
parallel lines:

1. *Kh*ândogya-upanishad V, 2, 6:
II. B*ri*had-âra*n*yaka, Mâdhyandina-sâkhâ, XIV, 9, 3,
10:
III. B*ri*had-âra*n*yaka-upanishad, Kâ*n*va-sâkhâ, VI, 3,
5:

I. Amo nâmâsy amâ hi te sarvam ida*m* sa hi *g*yesh*thah*
II. âmo 'sy âmam hi te mayi sa hi
III. âma*m*sy âma*m*hi te mahi sa hi

I. sresh*tho* râ*g*âdhipati*h* sa mâ *g*yaish*thyam s*rai-
II. râ*ge*sâno 'dhipati*h* sa mâ râ*ge*sâno
III. râ*ge*sâno

I. sh*thyam* râ*g*yam âdhipatya*m* gamayatv aham
eveda*m*
II. 'dhipati*m* karotv iti.
III. 'dhipati*m* karotv iti.

I. sarvam asânîti.
II.
III.

The text in the *Kh*ândogya-upanishad yields a certain
sense, viz. 'Thou art Ama by name, for all this together
exists in thee. He is the oldest and best, the king, the
sovereign. May he make me the oldest, the best, the
king, the sovereign. May I be all this.' This, according
to the commentator, is addressed to Prâ*n*a, and Ama,
though a purely artificial word, is used in the sense of
Prâ*n*a, or breath, in another passage also, viz. B*ri*had-

âranyaka-up. I, 3, 22. If therefore we accept this meaning of Ama, the rest is easy and intelligible.

But if we proceed to the Brihad-âranyaka, in the Mâdhyandina-sâkhâ, we find the commentator proposing the following interpretation: 'O Mantha, thou art a full knower, complete knowledge of me belongs to thee.' This meaning is obtained by deriving âmah from â + man, in the sense of knower, and then taking âmam, as a neuter, in the sense of knowledge, derivations which are simply impossible.

Lastly, if we come to the text of the Kânva-sâkhâ, the grammatical interpretation becomes bolder still. Sankara does not explain the passage at all, which is strange, but Ânandagiri interprets âmamsi tvam by 'Thou knowest (all),' and âmamhi te mahi, by 'we know thy great (shape),' which are again impossible forms.

But although there can be little doubt here that the reading of the Khândogya-upanishad gives us the original text, or a text nearest to the original, no sound critic would venture to correct the readings of the Brihad-âranyaka. They are corruptions, but even as corruptions they possess authority, at all events up to a certain point, and it is the fixing of those certain points or chronological limits, which alone can impart a scientific character to our criticism of ancient texts.

In the Kaushîtaki-brâhmana-upanishad Professor Cowell has pointed out a passage to me, where we must go beyond the text as it stood when commented on by the Sankarânanda. In the beginning of the fourth adhyâya all MSS. of the text read savasan, and this is the reading which the commentator seems anxious to explain, though not very successfully. I thought that possibly the commentator might have had before him the reading sa vasan, or so 'vasan, but both would be very unusual. Professor Cowell in his Various Readings, p. xii, conjectured sa*m*vasan, which would be liable to the same objection. He now, however, informs me that, as B. has sa*m*tvan, and C. satvan, he believes the original text to have been Satvan-Matsyeshu. This seems to me quite convincing, and is borne out by the reading of the Berlin MS., so far as it can be made out from Professor Weber's essay on the Upanishads, Indische Studien I, p.419. I see that Boehtlingk and Roth in their Sanskrit Dictionary, s*v*. satvat, suggest the same emendation.

The more we study the nature of Sanskrit MSS., the more, I believe, we shall feel convinced that their proper arrangement is one by locality rather than by time. I have frequently dwelt on this subject in the introductions to the successive volumes of my edition of the Rig-veda and its commentary by Sâya*n*âkârya, and my convictions on this point have become stronger ever since. A MS., however modern, from the south of India or from the north, is more important as a check on the textus receptus of any Sanskrit work, as prevalent in Bengal or Bombay, than ever so many MSS., even if of greater antiquity, from the same locality. When therefore I was informed by my friend Dr. Bühler that he had discovered in Kashmir a MS. of the Aitareya-upanishad, I certainly expected some real help from such a treasure. The MS. is described by its discoverer in the last number of the journal of the Bombay Asiatic Society, p. 34, and has since been sent to me by the Indian Government. It is written on birch bark (bhûrga), and in the alphabet commonly called Sârada. The leaves are very much injured on the margin and it is almost impossible to handle them without some injury. In many places the bark has shrunk, probably on being moistened, and the letters have become illegible. Apart from these drawbacks, there remain the difficulties inherent in the Sârada alphabet which, owing to its numerous combinations, is extremely difficult to read, and very trying to eyes which are growing weak. However, I collated the Upanishad from the Aitareya-âranyaka, which turned out to be the last portion only, viz. the Samhitâ-upanishad (Ait. Âr. III, 1-2), or, as it is called here, Samhitâranya, and I am sorry to say my expectations have been disappointed. The MS. shows certain graphic peculiarities which Dr. Bühler has pointed out. It is particularly careful in the use of the sibilants, replacing the Visarga by sibilants, writing s + s and s + s instead of h + s and h + s; distinguishing also the Gihvâmûlîya and Upadhmanîya. If therefore the MS. writes antastha, we may be sure that it really meant to write so, and not antahstha, or, as it would have written, antasstha. It shows equal care in the use of the nasals, and generally carries on the sandhi between different paragraphs. Here and there I met with better readings than those given in Rajendralal Mitra's edition, but in most cases the commentary would have been sufficient to restore the right reading. A few various readings, which seemed to deserve being mentioned, will be found in the notes. The MS., though carefully written, is not free from the ordinary blunders. At first one feels inclined to attribute some importance to every peculiarity of a new MS., but very soon one finds out that what seems peculiar, is in reality carelessness. Thus Ait. Âr. III, I, 5, 2, the Kashmir MS. has pûrvam aksharam rûpam, instead of what alone can be right, pûrvarûpam. Instead of pragayâ pasubhih it writes repeatedly pragaya pasubhih, which is impossible. In III, 2, 2, it leaves out again and again manomaya between khandomaya and vânmaya; but that this is a mere accident we learn later on, where in the same sentence manomayo, is found in its right place. Such cases reduce this MS. to its proper level, and make us look with suspicion on any accidental variations, such as I have noticed in my translation.

The additional paragraph, noticed by Dr. Bühler, is very indistinct, and contains, so far as I am able to find out, sânti verses only.

I have no doubt that the discovery of new MSS. of the Upanishads and their commentaries will throw new light on the very numerous difficulties with which a translator of the Upanishads, particularly in attempting a complete and faithful translation, has at present to grapple. Some of the difficulties, which existed thirty years ago, have been removed since by the general progress of Vedic scholarship, and by the editions of texts and commentaries and translations of Upanishads, many of which were known at that time in manuscript only. But I fully agree with M. Regnaud as to the difficultés considérables que les meilleures traductions laissent subsister, and which can be solved only by a continued study of the Upanishads, the Âranyakas, the Brâhmanas, and the Vedânta-sûtras.

THE *KHÂNDOGYA-UPANISHAD*.

THE *Kh*ândogya-upanishad belongs to the Sâma-veda. Together with the B*r*ihad-âra*n*yaka, which belongs to the Ya*g*ur-veda, it has contributed the most important materials to what may be called the orthodox philosophy of India, the Vedânta (1), i.e. the end, the purpose, the highest object of the Veda. It consists of eight adhyâyas or lectures, and formed part of a *Kh*ândogya-brâhma*n*a, in which it was preceded by two other adhyâyas. While MSS. of the *Kh*ândogya-upanishad and its commentary are frequent, no MSS. of the whole Brâhma*n*a has been met with in Europe. Several scholars had actually doubted its existence, but Rajendralal Mitra (2), in the Introduction to his translation of the *Kh*ândogya-upanishad, states that in India 'MSS. of the work are easily available, though as yet he has seen no commentary attached to the Brâhma*n*a portion of any one of them.' 'According to general acceptation,' he adds, 'the work embraces ten chapters, of which the first two are reckoned to be the Brâhma*n*a, and the rest is known under the name of *Kh*ândogya-upanishad. In their arrangement and style the two portions differ greatly, and judged by them they appear to be productions of very different ages, though both are evidently relics of pretty remote antiquity. Of the two chapters of the *Kh*ândogya-brâhma*n*a, the first includes eight sûktas (hymns) on the ceremony of marriage, and the rites necessary to be observed at the birth of a child. The first sûktas is intended to be recited when offering an oblation to

Agni on the occasion of a marriage, and its object is to pray for prosperity in behalf of the married couple. The second prays for long life, kind relatives, and a numerous progeny. The third is the marriage pledge by which the contracting parties bind themselves to each other. Its spirit may be guessed from a single verse. In talking of the unanimity with which they will dwell, the bridegroom addresses his bride, "That heart of thine shall be mine, and this heart of mine shall be thine." The fourth and the fifth invoke Agni, Vâyu, Kandramas, and Sûrya to bless the couple and ensure healthful progeny. The sixth is a mantra for offering an oblation on the birth of a child; and the seventh and the eighth are prayers for its being healthy, wealthy, and powerful, not weak, poor, or mute, and to ensure a profusion of wealth and milch-cows. The first sûkta of the second chapter is addressed to the Earth, Agni, and Indra, with a prayer for wealth, health, and prosperity; the second, third, fourth, fifth, and sixth are mantras for offering oblations to cattle, the manes, Sûrya, and divers minor deities. The seventh is a curse upon worms, insects, flies, and other nuisances, and the last, the concluding mantra of the marriage ceremony, in which a general blessing is invoked for all concerned.'

After this statement there can be but little doubt that this Upanishad originally formed part of a Brâhmana. This may have been called either by a general name, the Brâhmana of the Khandogas, the followers of the Sâma-veda, or, on account of the prominent place occupied in it by the Upanishad, the Upanishad-brâhmana. In that case it would be one of the eight

Brâhma*n*as of the Sâma-veda, enumerated by
Kumârila Bha*tta* and others (3), and called simply
Upanishad, scil. Brâhma*n*a.

The text of the Upanishad with the commentary of
*S*ankara and the gloss of Ânandagiri has been
published in the Bibliotheca Indica. The edition can
only claim the character of a manuscript, and of a
manuscript not always very correctly read.

A translation of the Upanishad was published, likewise
in the Bibliotheca Indica, by Rajendralal Mitra (4).

It is one of the Upanishads that was translated into
Persian under the auspices of Dârâ Shukoh, and from
Persian into French by Anquetil Duperron, in his
Oupnekhat, i.e. Secretum Tegendum. Portions of it
were translated into English by Colebrooke in his
Miscellaneous Essays, into Latin and German by F. W.
Windischmann, in his *S*ankara, seu de theologumenis
Vedanticorum. (Bonn, 1833), and in a work published
by his father, K. J. H. Windischmann, Die Philosophie
im Fortgang der Weltgeschichte (Bonn, 1827-34).
Professor A. Weber has treated of this Upanishad in
his Indische Studien I, 254; likewise M. P. Regnaud in
his Matériaux pour servir à l'histoire dc la philosophie
de l'Inde (Paris, 1876) and Mr. Gough in several
articles on 'the Philosophy of the Upanishads,' in the
Calcutta Review, No. CXXXI.

I have consulted my predecessors whenever there was
a serious difficulty to solve in the translation of these
ancient texts. These difficulties are very numerous, as

those know best who have attempted to give complete translations of these ancient texts. It will be seen that my translation differs sometimes very considerably from those of my predecessors. Though I have but seldom entered into any controversy with them, they may rest assured that I have not deviated from them without careful reflection.

Footnotes

1. Vedânta, as a technical term, did not mean originally the last portions of the Veda, or chapters placed, as it were, at the end of a volume of Vedic literature, but the end, i. e. the object, the highest purpose of the Veda. There are, of course, passages, like the one in the Taittirîya-âranyaka (ed. Rajendralal Mitra, p. 820), which have been misunderstood both by native and European scholars, and where vedânta means simply the end of the Veda:--yo vedâdau svarah prokto vedânte ka pratishthitah, 'the Om which is pronounced at the beginning of the Veda, and has its place also at the end of the Veda.' Here vedânta stands simply in opposition to vedâdau, and it is impossible to translate it, as Sâyana does, by Vedânta or Upanishad. Vedânta, in the sense of philosophy, occurs in the Taittirîya-âranyaka (p. 817), in a verse of the Narâyanîya-upanishad, repeated in the Mundaka-upanishad III, 2, 6, and elsewhere, vedântavignânasuniskitârah, 'those who have

well understood the object of the knowledge
arising from the Vedânta,' not 'from the last
books of the Veda;' and Svetâsvatara-up. VI, 22,
vedânte paramam guhyam, 'the highest mystery
in the Vedânta.' Afterwards it is used in the
plural also, e. g. Kshurikopanishad, 10 (Bibl.
Ind. p. 210), pundarîketi vedânteshu nigadyate,
'it is called pundarîka in the Vedântas,' i. e. in
the *Kh*ândogya and other Upanishads, as the
commentator says, but not in the last books of
each Veda. A curious passage is found in the
Gautama-sûtras XIX, 12, where a distinction
seems to be made between Upanishad and
Vedânta. Sacred Books, vol. ii, p. 272.

2. *Kh*ândogya-upanishad, translated by
   Rajendralal Mitra, Calcutta, 1862, Introduction,
   p. 17.
3. The same name seems, however, to be given to
   the adhyâya of the Talavakâra-brâhmana, which
   contains the Kena-upanishad.
4. M. M., History of Ancient Sanskrit Literature, p.
   348. Most valuable information on the literature
   of the Sâma-veda may be found in Dr. Burnell's
   editions of the smaller Brâhmanas of that Veda.

NOTES.

This text is a collaboration with:
O₂pen Windows: A Feminist Resource and Research Center.

O₂pen Windows is a feminist research cum *adda* center, based in Bangalore, India. If it could, it would sustain itself with endless cups of tea and lots of stimulating research.

The Purpose: We hope to open up the realm of religious discourse into the public domain of the secular; if we – the people – take these texts into our hands – then, we can do away with those parts that are misogynous and caste-ist and are fundamentally unconstitutional. We, the citizens, need to petition to the government to ensure that religious institutions comply with the laws of the land, and as India is a signatory to CEDAW – the nation complies with it and does not allow any institution (religious or otherwise) to violate it.

www.ingramcontent.com/pod-product-compliance
Lightning Source LLC
Chambersburg PA
CBHW060516030426
42337CB00015B/1905